FOUR STEP

Riding Success

KARIN BLIGNAULT

J.A. ALLEN · LONDON

First published in Great Britain in 2014

J. A. Allen
Clerkenwell House
Clerkenwell Green
London EC1R 0HT

J. A. Allen is an imprint of Robert Hale Limited
www.allenbooks.co.uk

ISBN 978-1-908809-14-8

British Library Cataloguing in Publication Data
A catalogue record for this book is available from the British Library

Design and typesetting by Paul Saunders
Edited by Martin Diggle

Photographs by the author and Richard Hodges, except for those on pages 23,
24 (right), 27 (top left and right) and 163 by Tracy Robertson, and those on pages 81,
147 and 162 by Johann Theron

Line drawings by Aike Smallberger

Printed in China by 1010 Printing International Ltd

Disclaimer of Liability

The author and publisher shall have neither liability nor responsibility to any
person or entity with respect to any loss or damage caused or alleged to be caused
directly or indirectly by the information contained in this book. While the book is as
accurate as the author can make it, there may be errors, omissions, and inaccuracies.

It is recommended that, whenever riding and whilst dealing with behavioural
problems in horses, a hard hat approved to current safety standards be worn.

CONTENTS

ACKNOWLEDGEMENTS

First I have to thank my generous husband who is prepared to endure years of neglected housework so that I can have the freedom to indulge my riding and writing. In thirty-five years of marriage he has not once complained about my horses. His support and encouragement, for me to follow my passions, are quite remarkable.

My gratitude also goes to my horses, my trainers and all my pupils who have each taught me so much – correct, but also incorrect applications. Without them there would not be even one book.

Thanks to my friends, Richard Hodges, Ewa and Slawek Rott-buga for their generous assistance with the photographs. A special thanks goes to Tracy Robertson for her beautiful photographs. Also thank you to my patient photographic model/pupils: Sarah, Michelle, Hayley, Kiara, Jodi and Libby. Thanks to Fiona Archer for her generous lending of her horse, Coal Miner, when I was forced to retire my beloved Papillon before we could take the necessary photographs.

To Aike Smallberger, who travelled many kilometres to patiently illustrate what I try to portray, thank you.

To physiotherapists Ulrike Hein, Nicola Ackerman and Janita Bellamy for being sounding boards on muscle use, Vanessa Harris for always being prepared to be a sounding board on all things horsy and Sandra Davids for reading the book, thank you. Thanks also to Anna Stępkowska for allowing me to use her analogy of ducks landing, and to Christi Bothma and Frances Dorer for their input.

I don't have the words to convey adequately my thanks to Sylvia Loch for finding time in her taxing schedule to write the Foreword for this book.

A special thanks to the Allen publishing team of Lesley Gowers, Martin Diggle and Paul Saunders for their wonderful work. It is always such a positive experience working with you.

FOREWORD BY SYLVIA LOCH

Most people will tell you they started riding because they loved horses. Whether it be the hairy pony at pasture, the athletic Warmblood in the stable, the sleek racehorse or jumper – there would be no motivation for our sporting activities if we did not admire horses and find sheer joy in being in the saddle. It was not so in times gone by; horses were a way of life – whether you liked them or not. Not only were they needed for transport, work in the field or battle; riding for pleasure was generally only for the very wealthy. It is unsurprising therefore that horse lore and equestrian education had to be crystal-clear and effective. If you did not make the right choices, you might lose your livelihood, or worse – your life.

Today, in the West, it is mostly equestrian sport that dominates our reasons for keeping horses. There are so many disciplines, all with their different rules and regulations; it must be very confusing for people embarking on their first experience of horses. Basic instruction is not always clear: anyone can teach riding and a certificate at the lowest rung of the ladder is of little value without years of experience behind it. When competition enters the picture, the divisions become more marked, and gurus abound in all the various disciplines. Even within the same discipline, one teacher says one thing, another something else, and yet another, the complete opposite! How can this be when Nature's laws are so unswerving? Reverting to Xenophon's early treatise of the fourth century BC, the principles of riding should be very clear and simple: the rider must be in as good a balance on horseback as when standing on the ground; a horse cannot operate to full potential or display his natural beauty when ridden with force. It is heartening that centuries later, these key precepts are still echoed today in the methodology of the great schools of equestrian art and by writers such as Karin Blignault.

As a trainer and a writer, I have been fortunate to learn from horses over five decades. I was taught the basic aids as a child but I remember the frustration of never being told 'how' we should do things and – just as important – 'why'. Sadly there was no Karin Blignault book to consult at the time, but at least I was blessed by good balance and good hands, so I muddled along. It was only when I went to Portugal in my early twenties, that some of the mystique of riding began to open up to me. Thanks to some wonderfully sensitive schoolmaster horses it dawned on me that the 'hows', the 'whys' and also the 'where's' could make all the difference to the horse's muscle systems and how he reacts to each and every aid. I also knew – as I had always guessed – that Xenophon was right. Position was all-important and any form of force could ruin the work.

In her writing, not only has Karin Blignault dealt with the very thorny question of gadgets and the perils of fixing the horse's neck and head; she has given us plenty of alternatives. It is easy to condemn the rollkurist or the person who rides their horse with an artificially shortened neck, but quite another to understand the effects and show the rider a better way. By clarifying so ably the biomechanics, how the horse reacts to pressure and how a rider may complement those automatic reactions and patterns of movement, Karin throws light on matters which for too long have remained hidden. Having devoured Karin's last book *Equine Biomechanics for Riders* and found it very supportive of my own convictions, I know many trainers will be greatly helped by this, her latest contribution.

As a teacher as well as a trainer, I know how important it is to understand all riders. Karin clearly knows the difficulties for those who are not necessarily 'feeling riders'. She offers logical strategies which will help build greater awareness and sensitivity in a practical way, step by step. I love the anecdotal glimpses which are drawn from life and which are all too familiar to every one of us who cares and wants the best for their students.

I believe this book has much to offer both novice riders and experts. We all need to remind ourselves that the make-up of the horse is very complex. Riding a horse is like tracing a journey in a very detailed road map. There are lots of ways, various options and avenues one can take – but too often one comes across a seemingly impassable point. What I love about Karin's work is how she shows us the clearest way, the one that works from a biomechanical point of view – in simple terms – Nature's way.

There will always exist a few differences between experts concerning the subtleties of riding, such as the seat, contact and weight aids but these can come down to interpretation of a particular situation or horse. For me, there is a vast difference between allowing our weight to drop, and intentionally weighting a seat bone or stirrup – when the pressures may change or vary. However, these niceties are very individual and there is little with which I would disagree in this book.

As Nuno Oliveira said: 'Riding is not just a sport, it is an art and a science and until we understand all three we can never truly call ourselves a horseman.' The longer I live the more I realise how true this is and I am very glad to add this book to my library.

AUTHOR'S NOTE

At various places in this text, I refer to the horse's 'natural movement', or how he 'moves in nature', and to modifications of such movement through the practice of dressage. In using this terminology, I'm aware of the possible inference that, if dressage modifies 'natural' movement it must therefore impose something 'unnatural'. There have, in the recent past, been certain training practices that at least come close to justifying this interpretation, so I want to explain briefly what I mean when I compare 'natural' movement with 'dressage' movement in this book.

The aims of dressage include improving the horse's understanding of what is required of him, and developing him physically so that he can carry the rider with greater ease and efficiency. It will be evident that it is not 'natural' for a horse to move with a rider on his back but, this being the case, there are various exercises and aiding combinations that can improve his strength, suppleness and balance under saddle. Such development is one of the primary aims of dressage and it should be seen as something very different from imposing an arbitrary 'outline' or way of going on the horse, for no reason except misplaced ego on the rider's part.

Where appropriate, brief explanations of the biomechanics involved in the horse's physical development are given in this book, but further detail can be found in my earlier book *Equine Biomechanics for Riders – The Key to Balanced Riding*.

My two chapters in this current book on use of the hands may seem extravagant and could be misinterpreted as teaching excessive hand use. However, in my many years of teaching, the most common problem I have experienced is the 'bad hand syndrome' (hanging, pulling, blocking) with the consequent defensive mouth problems in the horse. Correcting hand use is the most important aspect of training horses because riders tend to pull the hardest metal at the horse's most vulnerable point. Contact at even the highest levels of competition is often far too strong, with horses objecting by opening their mouths. Also, the methods explained in these chapters always increase leg awareness and use. This is a 'how to' book, which attempts to explain precise muscle action.

INTRODUCTION

THE SEEDS FOR THIS BOOK were sown many years ago, while I was grappling to comprehend the art of dressage. It developed through many frustrating and time-consuming years of struggling to understand trainers using vague and esoteric language of which both horse and rider had to second guess the meaning. They focused on correcting rider position, rather than teaching body use and effective control of the horse. Their only achievement was to tighten my body, causing the process to take longer. I realised that there was something fundamentally wrong in teaching this 'function follows form' method. My accidental path to teaching riding and my training in sports science and biomechanics have led me to follow the philosophy of teaching *body use* rather than focusing primarily on *body position*. By teaching riders how to apply their bodies in riding, their riding positions automatically become correct.

By combining theory and experimentation I finally developed a system of correcting my riding which was straightforward and fast. From my first book, *Successful Schooling – Ride Your Horse with Empathy*, this system developed progressively into a coherent and fast training and learning programme for both horse and rider.

I have read as many books on training as I can find, starting with Xenophon and continuing through the old masters, to today's most modern authors. The writers of the past were innovators, out-of-the-box thinkers, each with parts of the answer. They found solutions to their training problems through trial and error, feel and a passion for riding. They happily shared their knowledge with the world, sometimes despite vociferous criticism. Interspersed through all the books, we find a collective truth and much of what we know about horse training today. We have to assess and then accumulate the truths to piece the puzzle together. The books these masters wrote are the backbone of classical riding and should be used as a basis for finding the most effective current training techniques. However, most of these books focused on 'what to do' rather than 'how to do'.

Jean Saint-Fort Paillard wrote, 'Ideas and principles that previously have been accepted as fact have to go through continual re-examination of acquired knowledge'[1] and quoted the Comte d'Aure, who said, in the mid-nineteenth century: 'Dogma should not and cannot have a place in equestrian matters. It is high time for equestrian instruction to stop being dogmatic.'[2] Traditional teaching methods should thus go through re-examination to ensure that they keep up with modern sports science. New training techniques, such as rollkur/hyperflexion, should be examined scientifically to ensure that their biomechanical effects are not detrimental to horse or rider. We don't know what we don't know, and thus we readily believe that what we know is the whole truth, but this belief blocks progress. All the knowledge of both human and equine biomechanics is freely available today. This allows us to make a change in emphasis to incorporate modern sport science techniques into training horses, and teaching riders in a clearer, more objective language.

The dressage movements described in this book are ridden classically, but they are explained and taught through the sound biomechanical principle of human and equine movement. These principles include the effect of balance reactions, patterns of movement, movement through relaxation and the influence of gravity on movement. Rapid development of correct riding skills is the result of applying this knowledge. It took an eternity for me to reach Prix St Georges level in dressage because I was taught by the principle of function following form: communication with the horse was an utter mystery. It should take only three to four years to progress to this level when taught through the principles discussed in this book.

The art of riding is all about training horses to coordinate intricate new and protracted movement patterns and balance skills under the rider through clear, invisible communication. Arguably this clear language is the most important aspect of riding. Instructions should be explicit, unambiguous and with intent. When only one answer is possible, horses learn quickly and without confusion. Horses start reading riders the moment they are mounted. They read and try to follow each rider's inimitable movements and body language. By a trainer riding a horse straight after a pupil, the pupil's faults can be diagnosed immediately through the horse's 'new' reactions.

Good body use is essential for this explicit body language. After six thousand years of man's involvement with horses, the majority of riders are still ineffective at communicating clearly, despite the knowledge available, now augmented by research into sport science, neuromuscular science and learning theory! Phrases such as 'he knows', 'he won't', 'he is hanging on my hands', 'he runs away with me', 'he pops his shoulder', 'he is stubborn' or 'naughty' all place the responsibility of performance and learning on the horse. It is extremely unfair to expect a mere animal to take responsibility for inadequate rider communication. Horses and riders are written off as unable to progress when, in fact, all horses and riders, despite their weak areas (pathological issues excepted), are able to perform all the movements, even though the quality may not be to Olympic standard. When riders and trainers say that 'a horse can't', they are actually saying, 'I can't'. Horses are horses and will always react in the manner of the species. Riders have to take responsibility for the horse's understanding, and teachers, for the rider's understanding, no matter how 'complicated' the horse or rider.

The principle of function following form is generally accepted as the main training method today. This focus on position prevents riders from developing the coordination skills needed for exquisite communication. It is the reason for the misconception that learning takes a long time. We humans have gone through millions of years of evolution to ensure that we are exceptionally fast learners, provided we are taught correctly.

Problems or mistakes in riding are often tackled symptomatically with little success because symptoms are seldom the cause. Before jumping to conclusions at the first symptom of a fault, which is often the rider's seat, the origin of the biomechanical fault should be 'diagnosed'. Only then can it be corrected and the symptoms will disappear automatically. The cause of most riding and seat faults can usually be found in incorrect body use.

The 'hands without legs and legs without hands' method of riding is the only method which does not confuse horses. A common denominator in trainers who recommend this system is the often misunderstood François Baucher. He was one of the most innovative thinkers in the history of the sport. Unfortunately, he started off as a hard, demanding rider, using the unsound method of pushing the horse forwards into the hands discussed in Chapter 10, but this changed in time. He became a softer rider, promoting the 'hands without legs and legs without hands' method of training.

The messages this book highlights are: clear communication between teachers, riders and horses; the protection of the horse's mouth; and that learning to ride and train horses effectively should not take long.

Chapter 1

BASIC CONCEPTS

THE FOUR STEPS TO RIDING SUCCESS programme is based on equine and rider biomechanics. All riders can learn to influence and control the repertoire of movement possibilities that the horse shares with many quadrupeds in four easy exercises based on five responses to pressure. However, riders can only do this correctly if they have effective use of their own body.

THE FIVE PRIMARY RESPONSES REQUIRED FROM THE HORSE

All schooled movements are variations of the horse's five basic responses to the rider's requests. By eliciting these five responses correctly, riders have full control of the horse. These responses are:

1. The forward response.

2. The halt response.

3. The sideways response of the shoulders.

4. The sideways response of the hindquarters.

5. The independent head and neck bend response.

CONTROLLING THE WHOLE HORSE THROUGH KEY POINTS

The nineteenth-century French master François Baucher claimed that he could train a horse fully in seven hours. He believed that if he could control the horse's forehand and hindquarters, he had total control of the horse. For this purpose he did two exercises. The first was what he called flexions, in which he used the reins, in hand, to teach the horse to yield to rein pressure. The second exercise was the turn on the forehand, which taught the horse to yield to leg pressure. Today, over a century and a half later, the same principles hold true. However, Baucher was a riding genius and most riders need a little more than those two exercises for total control. Complete intricate command of the horse requires control of four key points. When you have complete control of these points, you can micro-manage all your horse's movements.

Key point of control	Effect
Control the head and neck	Suppleness, bend, balance, straightness, a consistent round, 'on the bit' frame and quality of action of the hindquarters
Control the shoulders	Straight on lines, circle size and lateral movements
Push the ribcage	Bend, straightness and balance
Control the hindquarters	All lateral work and engagement

The head

Control of the horse's head points his nose in the direction of the turn, circle, shoulder-in, half-pass and straight line. It directs his neck and governs bend, suppleness, straightness, balance and the quality of action of the hindquarters. The inside hand obtains neck bend and turns the horse's head. It assists in asking the horse to move into the rounded, 'on the bit' flexor frame. There is a difference however, between turning the horse and bending his head and neck. We have to learn to bend the horse's neck without affecting his turning shoulder movements. This ensures that he can continue straight without 'falling in'. Note that bending in the direction of the movement is not the horse's *automatic* method of turning. (See Author's Note.)

The shoulders

The outside rein controls the horse's shoulders. Control of the shoulders enables riders to:

- Ride straight on straight lines.

- Dictate and control the size of circles and turns.

- Control the sideways steps of lateral movements.

- Control the angle of the shoulder-in and the angle of the half-pass.

- Control the lateral steps of the walk and canter pirouettes.

- Prevent 'falling in' and 'falling out'.

IT TOOK ME ABOUT fifteen years to understand how the neck could be supple, flexible, yet fixed at the base or, as Erik Herbermann says, 'keep the neck laterally stable'. Finally I realised that the authors who wrote in these terms must have meant that the shoulders should be controlled to prevent them from 'falling out or in' with the consequent excessive lateral bending of the neck. Excessive neck bend disappears when the shoulders are controlled.

The ribcage

The legs, in the girth area on the ribcage, control bend and affect balance significantly. Inside leg pressure on the ribcage shifts it and pushes the horse's weight to his outside legs. It elicits a balance reaction which produces bend. It prevents the horse from 'falling' on his inside shoulder throughout turns, circles and lateral work.

The hips

The legs, well behind the girth, on the bulge of the horse's abdomen, control the horse's hindquarters. This produces lateral movement of the hind legs.

The rider's body

Effective body use is essential for clear communication. This ensures that the horse does not receive mixed signals or opposing messages. Effective body use is reliant on an independent seat. An independent seat consists of three important elements:

1. Independent balance

2. Independent fine motor coordination

3. Independent gross motor coordination

FOUNDATION MOVEMENTS

Two movements form the foundation of all the other dressage movements up to Grand Prix level, which are thus variations of these two training tools. They are also used to improve the quality of all the schooling movements because they encourage engagement of the hindquarters and the correct bend. Both are essential for balance in high-level dressage work and in jumping. They are also the key to the rider learning effective body use and effective communication with the horse. They are thus arguably the most important movements for horses and riders to master. They are:

1. The half-halt

2. The shoulder-in

It is difficult for both the novice horse and the novice rider to master the coordination required for the half-halt and the shoulder-in. Therefore they have to be chunked down into their constituent parts. The building blocks of the half-halt are the halt and forward steps. The building block of the shoulder-in is the ability to ride in a straight line with a slight inside bend – the 'bent-straight' position.

BODY LANGUAGE

Horses will perform every task correctly, provided the request is communicated in a manner which they can understand immediately. The medium for this two-way communication between horse and rider is body language. This language is dependent on three well-developed fields of awareness for both horse and rider:

1. Feel perception

2. Technique and timing

3. Anticipation

FOUR STEPS TO RIDING SUCCESS

Four basic steps cover all that is needed for both horse and rider to learn the above-mentioned skills. These skills will take riders to the highest dressage level and/or turn them into competent jumpers.

1. Learning the technique of giving light forward aids and teaching the horse to respond to light forward aids.

2. Learning to coordinate light halt aids and teaching the horse to halt from light leg aids.

3. Learning to coordinate the aids for lateral movements and teaching the horse to yield and take lateral steps from light aids.

4. Learning to control the horse's shoulders by maintaining a straight line together with bend. Teaching the horse to maintain balance while moving straight with a bend.

(The reasons for, and explanations of how to develop the feel and coordination needed to achieve this are explained in the following chapters.)

Chapter 2

TEACHING
NEW MOVEMENTS

Bοτη riders and horses learn new movements faster when riders understand the methodology of learning new physical activities.

TEACHING THE CONCEPT

The best methods of teaching horses new aids ('words') are essentially the same as when teaching children new words.

1. **Explain and teach the basic concept.** This is done by manoeuvring the horse into the correct position and eliciting his automatic reactions for an immediate correct response. For example, the initial halts do not need to be square so long as the horse understands that he should be motionless. In the simple change the horse has to understand that he must move from canter to walk, not canter to trot to walk. If he is allowed to trot into the walk, he will assume that the trot is what is required. The trot will be reinforced and learning will take longer. It does not matter if the initial flying changes are late behind (this is how he does the change in nature), so long as the horse understands the requirement to change on command. Initially, shoulder-in does not have to be fully 'on the bit', but the horse must understand fundamentally that his hind limbs have to stay on the track while his shoulders move in from the track.

2. **Repeat the explanations until the concept/movement is understood to the extent that it becomes a familiar memory.** The 'explanations' become a signal (aid) which elicits the correct reaction instantly.

3. **Once the horse understands the *concept*, refine the movement.** For example, teach the horse to halt square in front; teach the horse to change fore and hind legs simultaneously in the flying changes. (Persistent faults in flying changes are usually caused by inadequate rider timing); add the round flexor 'on the bit' frame to the shoulder-in and the simple changes.

4. **When all the pieces are put together, add engagement and collection to the movement.** Collect the movement before the halt and ask for all four legs to square-up. Collect the canter in and out of the walk. Collect the canter into the flying changes and ask for a big 'jump'. Add impulsion and more engagement in the shoulder-in.

The development of the sample movements mentioned is summarised in the table below.

Halt	Simple change	Flying change	Shoulder-in
Not square	Abrupt	Change in front first	Angle without flexor frame or correct bend
Square in front	Smooth and balanced, with correct frame	Clean changes front and back	Angle with flexor frame and bend
All four feet square	Collected in and out	Collect with expression	Add rhythm and impulsion

Chunking the movement

The rider

The most economical method of learning to coordinate complex new patterns of movement is to 'chunk' them into their constituent parts or smallest units. Each part is learnt separately and once each section can be performed with ease, the pieces are all put together to produce the new, complex coordinated movement. Compare this to an orchestra playing a symphony. The music for each instrument is learnt and practised individually until perfect. Following this, each group of identical instruments, say violins, practise until perfect. Finally the whole orchestra is put together into a complex synchronised symphony, each instrument essential for a fluent performance.

To take an example from riding, let's look at learning the coordination for riding the shoulder-in by breaking it into its constituent parts.

1. First learn to vibrate the inside rein while maintaining a light contact on the outside rein.

2. Learn to separate your leg movements. Push with your inside leg while your outside leg learns to be completely passive.

3. Learn to dissociate your inside hand and leg movements.

4. Move the horse's shoulder in with your outside arm, not by pulling on the inside rein. Pulling on the inside rein creates a false bend – see Chapter 7.

5. Use finger vibrations on the inside or on both reins to explain to the horse to move into a round flexor 'on the bit' frame.

6. Learn to use your inside seat muscles to push the horse laterally.

7. Learn to use your inside abdominal oblique muscles to push the horse laterally (see illustration on page 142).

8. Learn to give forward aids with your seat muscles and inside leg.

Each of these muscle actions has to be repeated until your coordination is perfect. When each section is perfect, all the separately learnt actions are put together. All your limbs now perform their individual actions (the aids) to form the whole coordinated pattern of movement for a good shoulder-in.

LESLEY'S HORSE SPEEDED up after each flying change. The changes also lacked quality. She was not coordinated enough to ask for the change, soften the reins for the horse to 'jump' and then follow up immediately with walk to prevent the speeding up. The first step was to ask for the walk immediately after the change. Once the horse learnt to 'hesitate' after the change, the rider could allow her hands forward to encourage the horse to jump through. The next step was to collect the horse immediately after the change stride.

The horse

Horses do not understand complex non-verbal instructions. Each new movement has to be developed in small steps, chunking it into its constituent parts. Teach the horse each bite-size piece separately. Only add the next part when the previous one becomes easy. If a mistake creeps in, go back to the previous step and repeat many times until the horse can perform it correctly. The horse will drop his neck and soften his eye when he is ready to proceed to the next step. For example, assuming that the horse has done the Four Steps programme as described in Chapter 7, teach him the shoulder-in in the following small steps.

1. Start the movement at the walk.

2. As you go through the corner onto the long side, push the horse's hindquarters into the corner with your inside leg.

3. Move his shoulders to the inside, with your outside rein, as you come out of the corner.

4. Continue pushing with your inside leg at every stride and add finger vibrations with your inside hand to maintain a slight inside bend.

5. Ask for the round flexor 'on the bit' frame with finger pressure and release on either the inside rein or alternate reins.

6. Maintain the angle by keeping your outside hand steady when the angle is correct.

7. Trot the movement.

CONTROLLING MOVEMENT THROUGH BODY LANGUAGE

Biomechanical understanding, of horses specifically, has helped us through the centuries to develop an extremely effective communication system. This system is based on the control of the horse's automatic reactions. The following concepts highlight these reactions. However, for a more detailed explanation of equine biomechanics, you can read my previous book, *Equine Biomechanics for Riders – The Key to Balanced Riding*.

The prototype of the motor car

The horse and carriage were arguably the prototype of the motor car. The horse's head is the steering wheel. It points him in the correct direction. The reins are the levers to the steering wheel. If our arms were long enough we would be holding onto and steering with the bit. This is the reason why the connection between the reins and the hands should be solid. They should not slip, but form a consistent straight line to the rider's elbows.

The horse's hindquarters are the engine, which should be 'ignited' from behind. It pushes the forehand forwards. His forelimbs are his natural brakes which push

far left As you go through the corner onto the long side, push the horse's hindquarters into the corner with your inside leg.

left Move his shoulders to the inside, with your outside rein, as you come out of the corner.

below left Continue pushing with your inside leg at every stride and add finger vibrations with your inside hand to maintain a slight inside bend.

below centre Ask for the round flexor 'on the bit' frame with finger pressure and release on either the inside rein or alternate reins.

below right Maintain the angle by keeping your outside hand steady when the angle is correct.

The five photos above: Introducing shoulder-in.

into the ground to stop while he lifts his neck to balance by moving his centre of gravity back. In dressage we ride the horse in the round 'on the bit' frame which gives us better engagement and control of the horse. However, this round frame prevents the horse from using his neck for balance and pushing his weight onto his forelimbs for braking. He thus has to use his hind legs to brake by bending their joints and pushing them into the ground – like a duck landing. This ensures that he can maintain a consistent round frame during transitions.

Riding the horse 'forwards into the contact' causes bit pressure in his mouth. Horses understand bit pressure as a stopping instruction just as the brake pedal stops the car. (The bit does not cause undue pressure if the horse is in self-carriage.) Simultaneous leg pressure would tell the horse to use his engine at the same time. If we maintain pressure on the car's accelerator and on the brake pedals simultaneously both the engine and the brakes may burn out. This is exactly what happens to horses when we give simultaneous going and stopping aids. Their mouths harden and they stop moving forwards.

The horse's four limbs are the wheels. There is no point in turning the steering wheel if the wheels do not react. We have to control the horse's shoulders if we want to 'turn his wheels'.

BIOMECHANICAL REACTIONS

Automatic reactions

Animals move because of automatic reactions and automatic patterns of movement. If we can teach the horse by manoeuvring him, using these automatic reactions and patterns, he will understand us the first time we ask for an action and thus remember and repeat this correct reaction ever after. This method cuts considerable time off training. All the aids which have developed naturally over the centuries of riding are based on eliciting and manoeuvring these basic reactions. For example, if we position the horse and prepare him correctly for the canter, he will take the correct lead on the first request (unless there is an underlying pathology preventing it) – see Chapter 4.

It is important to understand that all ambulatory movement in all animals (except, sometimes, backward movement) is initiated by the *head,* not by the *hindquarters.* You can demonstrate this to yourself by carrying out the following exercises.

1. Stand up from a sitting position then turn to the side. Take note of how your head initiated both movements.

2. Stand with your head and back against a wall. Take a forward step. Take note of which body part left the wall first.

3. Walk forwards without leaning forwards, pressing up on your toes or leaning forwards from your ankles. Take note of how clumsy it feels to lead the movement with your feet.

Horses initiate movement in the same manner – with their heads and necks. They move their necks forward first when taking a forward step. They lift their necks when taking backward steps. When turning to the side at walk, they generally first look in the direction, then take the lateral step. However, because of the position of their eyes, they can see to the sides without turning their heads. In trot and canter they generally counterbalance their sideways-stepping turn by moving their heads and necks to the opposite side.

The round flexor 'on the bit' frame is initiated by the head in all animals. Flexing of the neck produces contraction of the abdominal muscles, which round and lift the back. This leads to contraction of the hip flexors which, in the horse's case, brings the horse's hindquarters underneath his body.

The hollow extensor frame is also initiated by the horse's head and neck, and this hollowing is really only observable in the horse's neck. The rigidity of the horse's back prevents us from observing the hollowing into the extensor frame.* However, the muscle tone in all the topline muscles increases to produce this 'hollow' back.

In nature, the horse generally bends his neck to the outside in counterbalance when turning at trot or canter.

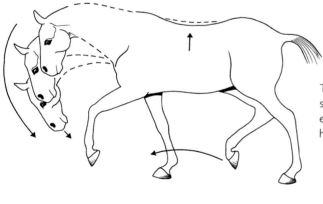

The round flexor frame starts at the head and ends with flexion of the hind legs.

* *Note* A distinction should be drawn between the extensor (hollow) frame or pattern, when the horse comes above the bit (as also seen in the 'startle reflex') and the gait extensions, in which the horse takes longer strides, in a longer outline, but is not 'hollow'.

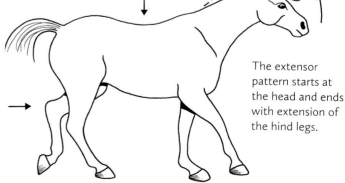

The extensor pattern starts at the head and ends with extension of the hind legs.

Balance reactions

Pushed from behind, we automatically take forward steps. Pushed from the side we automatically take sideways steps and pushed from the front we automatically take backward steps. These are automatic balance reactions to ensure that our centres of gravity are maintained above our bases of support. This principle also applies to horses.

Automatic protective balance reactions are fast, but learning new dynamic balance develops from slow to fast until it becomes automatic. Think of the gymnasts on the balance beam. They start slowly, first finding their balance standing still. Then they take small steps and eventually they run and tumble.

In nature the horse works in an extended frame with his head and neck straight and his hindquarters in extension. This is for fast flight. His balance is good because he knows where he is going. He is in control of his own footfall. The ridden horse not only has to contend with a new controlling object on his back (which does not always give clear instructions) but also with being pushed forwards in an unnatural frame (often being restricted in the mouth) – see Author's Note at start of book.

The horse uses his head and neck to maintain balance and to move his centre of gravity over his base of support. The horse's centre of gravity in normal circumstances is roughly at the position of the rider's knees. He moves it forwards by stretching his neck forwards. He moves it back by lifting his neck. He moves it to the side by moving his shoulder sideways. In the last scenario, he has to move his neck to the opposite side to counterbalance. This shows clearly that the horse uses his neck to maintain balance. Thus, when he lifts his neck and hollows in downward transitions, this is not resistance, but a balance reaction. When he loses his bend while he moves his shoulder inwards on turns and circles, it is not

below left The natural frame.

below right The 'dressage' frame.

necessarily through a lack of suppleness, but is often a balance reaction. The only method of preventing hollowing in downward transitions is to ask the horse to move into the round flexion pattern first, then to ask for the downward transition slowly to allow him to shift his balance reactions to his hindquarters and to maintain balance with them. If we want the horse to bend we have to push his ribcage with unilateral leg pressure. This is not 'stepping in', but pushing more weight on his outside legs to enable bend. His automatic reaction will turn his head towards your pushing leg – thus the inside bend is established.

This young horse is incorrectly bent owing to a balance reaction, not a lack of suppleness. He is turning naturally with his weight on his inside legs and his neck bending out.

Try the following exercises to illustrate balance reactions.

1. Walk on a ground pole and notice how your arms work like a balance pole to maintain your balance. The horse uses his neck like a balance pole.

2. Walk on a ground pole with folded arms. Notice how difficult it is to balance without using your arms. It is as difficult for the horse to balance without using his neck.

3. Walk on a ground pole but push your stomach out, dropping your weight into your hips and stabilising them. Imagine a blow-up ball expanding in your pelvic area. This lowers your centre of gravity. Horses, too, use their hips and bend their hind legs for balance when they are prevented from using their heads and necks in the 'on the bit' position.

I HAVE VERY RECENTLY COME to realise that countless training problems stem from asking the horse to balance through circles and bending movements in a manner that is the opposite of his natural method of placing his weight on his inside shoulder and moving his head to the outside in trot and canter. In dressage we bend him in the direction of his turns and circles, thus changing his natural balance. This has to be done with care to prevent the horse 'falling in' and losing bend and balance. Bending in the direction of movement improves suppleness and balance.

This is the reason why many of the great masters spent so much time on establishing bend. For example, Steinbrecht achieved this by means of the so-called ribcage bend,[1] focusing on the horse stepping forward with his inside hind leg. This is lateral flexion, or 'bend'. For L'Hotte, straightness was 'the foundation of educated equitation'.[2] He claimed that, when losing straightness, the horse's shoulder falls in and that lateral flexion – 'bend' – corrects it. This 'falling in' is the difficulty of bending in the direction of going, which is against the horse's natural inclination. Kurt Albrecht described it as 'natural crookedness'[3] in which the horse's shoulder falls in, and saw it as a major issue that had to be addressed by astute schooling.

PATTERNS OF MOVEMENT

This subject has been covered extensively in *Equine Biomechanics – The Key to Balanced Riding*. However, a short description is added for the reader's convenience.

Bodies move in organised systems of movement patterns in a cephalo-caudal (head to tail) direction. This means that movement of the head and neck affect the entire horse. Riders should thus initiate flexion from the horse's head until he understands the concept, after which he may associate certain leg pressures with the correct head and neck actions. Horses have limited possibilities of movement patterns because their legs have to be maintained as support structures underneath their large and heavy torso. Their basic patterns of movement are established before birth.

The flexor pattern starts with the horse's head and neck flexor muscles which round his neck. This is followed by contraction of his abdominal muscles, followed by his hip flexors. Rounding his head and neck is thus the start of engagement of the hindquarters into the round flexor 'on the bit' frame.

The extensor pattern starts with the horse's head and neck hollowing into extension. This is followed by contraction of the back muscles, followed by the hip extensors. The hollow extension pattern thus disengages the hindquarters.

The lateral flexion pattern starts with the head and neck bending to the side. This is followed by contraction of his side muscles.

The rotational pattern starts with a twisting of the head and neck. Horses usually use this pattern when getting up from lying down and when biting an itch on the rump. A twisting head (rotation of the head) in lateral movements is often caused by too strong an outside rein, or a balance reaction.

above left The flexor pattern, showing flexor muscle contraction from the head and neck through the abdominals to the hindquarters.

left The hollow extensor pattern.

above right The lateral flexion pattern in half-pass, showing lateral flexor muscle contraction.

The equine neck reaction

The equine neck reaction (ENR) is an automatic reaction peculiar to rigid-backed quadrupeds. It is a very important concept when training horses because neck movements influence the horse's hindquarters.

When the horse's neck tightens, his entire spinal column becomes a rigid unit. If the rider pulls on a tight inside rein to turn or to bend instead of asking the horse to yield to the rein pressure, his hindquarters will swing out in a straight line to the opposite side, like a ship turning.

We can use the influence of the ENR on hind leg movements to our advantage by using it in some movements while inhibiting it in others.

- If you need your outside leg to prevent the hindquarters from swinging out in the shoulder-in, half-pass, walk and canter pirouettes, and flying changes, the horse is not yielding correctly to inside rein pressure. Using your leg to prevent the quarters from swinging removes the symptom, not the cause. It is like taking an antihistamine for a cold; it does not take the cold away. There is thus no point in pushing the hindquarters back with your leg. You have to inhibit this reaction to prevent the hindquarters from swinging out by asking the horse to maintain a soft bend with finger vibrations.

- Straighten a crooked rein-back by tightening the rein on the side to which the horse is moving crookedly. His hindquarters will move to the opposite side if his spine works as a unit. You can control the direction of each backward step in this manner.

- In leg-yield, move your outside rein closer to the horse's neck, in the direction of your opposite hipbone (back and over). This action moves his hindquarters laterally. You then need less leg pressure. This concept is explained in detail in Chapter 7.

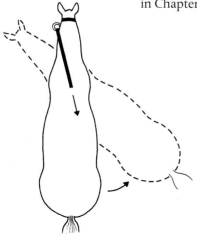

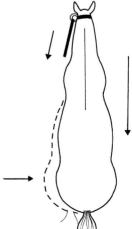

left The equine neck reaction, in which the hindquarters swing out if the horse does not yield to rein pressure.

right Straighten the rein-back with the equine neck reaction.

- The ENR is often used, incorrectly and unwittingly, as an aid to encourage the horse to move his hindquarters in the turn on the forehand by pulling the rein on the side of the pushing leg (see Chapter 7).

Exercises to demonstrate communication through manoeuvring the horse's automatic reactions

Knowing how to manoeuvre the horse's automatic movement patterns, through the four key points of control, assists riders to position the horse correctly when training all riding movements. It removes confusion.

The automatic reactions enable us to influence the horse's bend, the use of his abdominal muscles, his balance, and his hindquarters through control of his head.

Use a partner to experiment a little with this non-verbal body language which we should use to communicate with our horses. Use only your hands placed on either side of your partner's ribs.

- Ask her/him to walk forwards for a few steps by pushing forwards.

- Ask for the 'halt' by pushing your hands in, locking your elbows and stopping.

- Push to the side and slightly forwards to convince your partner to walk sideways, crossing one leg in front of the other.

- Push sideways and slightly backwards to convince your partner to walk sideways by crossing one leg behind the other.

- Convince your partner to walk backwards by pulling back.

These exercises demonstrate exactly how horses understand and misunderstand us. We can make people walk with their toes pointing in and also with their toes pointing out, by simply manoeuvring their weight and automatic reactions.

right I turn Jodie's hip in while I push it forwards to make her walk with her toes pointing in.

far right I turn Jodie's hip out while I push her leg forwards to make her walk with her toes pointing out.

Chapter 3

BODY USE AND
THE INDEPENDENT SEAT

The importance of a correct seat lies in its effectiveness. A classical and correct seat is necessary for competition dressage, but it has to remain dynamic because a static position blocks forward movement. A perfect position does not, however, *guarantee* true effectiveness and is of little value if it is not accompanied by good body use. If riders cannot coordinate their bodies to aid their horses with clarity, how can they expect their horses to understand their instructions? Only with good body use can riders communicate clear, unambiguous instructions (aids) to the horse in a way in which each horse can understand.

That said, however, the ideal posture and seat on a horse does ultimately place the rider in the best position for effective body use. For example, a rider cannot use his or her seat muscles to improve the canter if those muscles are not in good contact with the saddle. Leaning forward takes the seat out of the saddle. (Of course, to continue the point made above, if the seat muscles are in good contact with the saddle, but the rider does not use them to improve the canter, the canter will not improve.) Similarly, the simple fact of sitting upright in the canter will not engage the hindquarters, and neither does sitting upright bring the horse off his forehand or prevent him from 'falling' on his forehand. It is good body use which prevents or corrects the problem.

Good body use is the ability, when necessary, to coordinate the muscle actions of a particular body part without it affecting the independent actions of another body part. This is a prerequisite for an effective and independent seat. It means that the body can multi-task, move in harmony with the horse and communicate well. Both horses and humans are body coordination problem-solvers. The more input they are given, the faster they can solve their body-use problems. Effective body use should thus be taught to riders from the outset of learning to ride. It is the fastest way to develop an independent and correct seat.

FORM FOLLOWS FUNCTION

It is often assumed that, so far as the rider's position is concerned, function follows form. This perception, which is often articulated in the form that the rider can only be effective with a perfectly correct classical seat, is an oversimplification. Some imperfections in postural alignment will not necessarily hinder effectiveness. Less-than-perfect riding postures are often seen in very effective riders in the showjumping and cross-country disciplines and sometimes, also, in dressage. Small flaws such as rounded shoulders and turned-in hands are examples. François Baucher has been described as 'the most exceptional equestrian genius of all times',[1] yet his seat and posture were questionable:

> His torso was short, his thighs rather fleshy and his head was bent over forwards almost touching his chest. His legs and feet were thrust back. He moved in his seat when he and his horse executed lead changes [his] legs always gripped the horse's flanks and were placed so far back that his torso was pushed forwards, where the weight of his head already inclined it to go.[2]

Yet he achieved superior lightness and developed many of the concepts used in competition dressage today.

The belief that function follows form may produce riders with perfect riding postures, but this is not always accompanied by effectiveness. Learning to ride by instructions to position the body generally leads to rigidity, with the consequent loss of relaxed movement. The body tightens, especially in the areas of the arms and shoulder girdle. A forced, tight position may appear correct, but it prevents effective body use. It has led to generations of riders giving their horses simultaneous forward and stopping instructions. Rigidity is always perceived by the horse as a stopping instruction. It blocks forward movement and hardens his mouth. Unless there is underlying pathology, mouth problems are always caused by incorrect riding techniques. Focusing on rider position rather than on communication with the horse can only result in ineffective control. This does not, however, mean that riders should *ignore* postural and seat imperfections.

To sum up the relationship between correct, aesthetically pleasing posture and effective riding, we can look at the views of two masters of the past. Wilhelm Müseler said that the conception of a so-called 'correct seat' is the source of a dangerous over-estimation of the value of external appearance, and has done a lot of damage ... but it must never be forgotten that the rider's position is in every smallest detail determined by the influence he wants to exert on the horse. And here again, both 'seat' and 'influence' are determined by the 'feel'.[3]

The great Gustav Steinbrecht believed that good position was of no use unless the rider could also be effective. He said:

Many riding schools and riding instructors train riders that carry themselves in a dainty position, but they are unable to teach them to regulate the carriage and gait of their horses .... It is necessary to give a student the necessary steadi-ness and posture to prevent him from sitting on the horse like a farmer, but one should not take away the agility of his limbs with which he can instinctively feel the rhythm of the gaits and thus the proper moment for giving an aid.[4]

In Western riding too, the emphasis is on effectiveness, as stated by Charlene Strickland: 'You don't need to look perfect. You just ride efficiently. In most Western riding, you ride for function rather than form.'[5]

Unfortunately, the seat position often seems to be overemphasised in training, to the point of neglect of rider effectiveness and the development of feel and body use. The belief that the seat makes the rider (function follows form) also prevents the diagnosis of the real riding problem. The trainer continues to work on the rider's seat, but the underlying coordination problem remains. Finding the com-bined horse and rider biomechanics of the problem and correcting body use, rather than rider position, is the only effective method of solving riding problems.

DURING A RECENT LUNGE lesson with an 8-year-old boy, the teacher was giving him the usual riding school instructions for rising trot. 'Sit down', 'shoul-ders back', 'heels down', 'hands up' and 'elbows back'. This is teaching body position and can only cause rigidity, especially in an anxious rider. During the canter without stirrups his upper body moved ever forward while his lower legs moved far back. The teacher instructed him 'not to lean forwards, because it was causing his legs to move back'. The real cause of his problem was anxiety, which caused knee gripping and his upper body to move forwards. These reac-tions loosened his lower legs and moved them back. No amount of instruction on position will correct the fault while the rider's body is in protective rigidity. These problems disappear when riders are taught balance and coordination – body use – rather than body position.

A neat position, but with rigid arms causing mouth pressure and defensive behaviour in the first lesson.

In the second lesson the relaxed arms soften the bit pressure. The horse thus relaxes and yields.

Many postural faults are caused by ineffective body use and what are termed 'associated movements'. The latter – extraneous movements that appear automatically when learning complex physical skills – are explained in more detail later in this chapter. As coordination, balance and feel improve through training, the limbs learn to move independently and effectiveness improves. This leads to automatic corrections of posture and seat – in other words, form following function.

The sequence of photos below shows how a rider progressed from incoordination to good body use and posture in three lessons.

It is easy to teach the rider the perfect position on a correctly trained horse. However, under certain circumstances, it may be of more value to temporarily sacrifice the aesthetically ideal position and posture for a seat with perfect timing and effective body use.

top left Rising trot, lesson one: the rider's arms are rigidly bent and the horse is reacting by pulling against bit pressure. Long-limbed riders often take up this position with their elbows protruding behind their back.

top right Rising trot, lesson three: relaxed and balanced with the rider's centre of gravity over her base of support, allowing elastic contact.

below left Turn on the forehand, lesson one: complete lack of coordination.

below centre Turn on the forehand, lesson two: rider in balance with much improved body use, but has not added the round flexor frame to the movement.

below right Turn on the forehand, lesson three. Rider balanced and relaxed and can multi-task while maintaining a good position, with the horse 'on the bit'.

Learning new movements

Attempting to maintain the correct posture, while learning the coordination for new movements, often leads to incorrect body use which slows down the learning process. It creates unnecessary frustration and interferes with rider-horse communication and training. Novice riders easily lose their posture when they are learning the necessary gross and fine motor coordination, balance and control needed for an independent seat. They also lose posture when learning new techniques and new movements, especially when attempting to teach their own horses new movements such as the shoulder-in. Some novice riders may only be capable of maintaining a round frame by holding their hands wide apart. Bert Rutten says, 'I educate the rider's seat by progressing the rider's experience, and as the horse comes into better balance the rider's position becomes better.'[6]

A novice rider's posture is often lost when incorrect techniques are used in an attempt to maintain impulsion on a sluggish horse. In the effort to move the horse forwards, the rider's shoulders may round and the abdominal muscles contract. Riders may resort to kicking the horse's sides continuously, or bounce in the saddle in an attempt to move the horse. These problems disappear fast when the correct techniques are used instead of focusing on position.

far left This rider is leaning over in shoulder-in in an attempt to push the horse sideways.

left Rider sitting upright in the shoulder-in after being shown how to use her hamstring and leg adductor muscles and her abdominal oblique muscles.

Training young horses

Riders also often lose their posture while training young, unschooled horses, or when retraining incorrectly schooled horses. Communicating their requests to the horse needs to be immediately effective to avoid confusion. Damaged horses may respond better with the rider's hands used wide apart. Young horses are often trained in a light seat and with hands held apart. Gustav Steinbrecht had the following to say about the rider's position when training a green horse:

> However, to achieve this [light and elastic seat and light and steady hand], he must often depart from the regularly accepted body posture and hand position, and it is therefore a sign of great ignorance if the public judges his work only by the position of his body … The expert rider should be judged only by the results of his work … more yet by the performance of that horse than by his own position.[7]

AFTER A YEAR'S ABSENCE from seeing me ride, a friend remarked that my position had improved dramatically. The answer was quite simple. I had not worked on my position at all, but had finally become effective in coordinating my body, and thus the horse. No exertion was necessary to guide the horse and therefore it was easy to ride with good posture. I had learnt the function, and the form followed automatically.

Practical considerations and rider safety

It is not always practical to learn to be simultaneously effective as well as to sit perfectly. Effectiveness should take precedence over seat and postural inaccuracies because riding is potentially extremely dangerous. Maintaining the correct seat and posture is difficult when anxiety is involved. Anxiety dissipates as balance, coordination, body use and control of the horse develop.

The classical schools advocate many hours of lungeing to develop a perfect seat. The correct position and good balance are often taught in riding schools. These two methods, however, neglect the development of fine and gross motor-coordination. Teaching coordination and feel together with balance develops independence and a correct seat far faster than focusing first on the 'perfect' seat.

Steinbrecht recommends:

> directing the student, as soon as he has become somewhat secure, to work on his horse's carriage, although this might once in a while occur at the expense of his normal position … I believe, the fact that this 'normal' seat is demonstrated

to the student right at the beginning and is practised with great discipline, is the main reason why many young people are frightened away from the arena and from the systematic study of the art of riding. Instead, they prefer the unrestrained and exclusive riding of hunts and steeplechases, although with suitable instruction they might have become higher-level dressage riders.[8]

This still seems to be true today, insofar that most riders choose the less constricted showjumping, cross-country and hunting arenas and where Natural Horsemanship is gaining followers by the day.

WHILE WATCHING A truly effective FEI trainer, with a far-from-correct posture, correcting clients' horses, a spectator commented that 'effective riders know precisely how to use their hands and arms'. Another trainer's response, however, was that novice riders and beginners should not be taught to use their hands because they lack the coordination and balance and may pull the horse in the mouth.

The fact is, that when novice riders are not taught the necessary coordination and balance from the outset, the results are always the same: pulling, rigid, unyielding arms and hands, resulting in mouth problems in the horse.

Virtually every time I walk past a riding lesson, I hear the refrain: 'Heels down, straighten your shoulders' and the worst two instructions of all, 'Hold your hands still' and 'Keep your elbows by your sides'. These instructions all cause rigidity and are not how coordination, balance and control are learnt. They teach nothing. Riders (novices and beginners) should learn to move, coordinate and communicate with their hands to develop an independent seat. Perfecting the rider's position and posture should not be an end in itself: it should rather be a means by which to influence the horse in the most effective manner.

The correct seat plus effectiveness, is the ultimate goal. Teaching coordination and effective body use automatically leads to good posture because the coordinated rider's body becomes relaxed, is able to control and communicate with the horse easily, and is free of associated movements.

THE INDEPENDENT SEAT

Our two primary objectives when learning to ride are, first, not to fall off and second, to control the horse by making ourselves understood. For the first, we need balance, but for the second we need independent body use. An independent seat is thus determined by the development of independent and automatic balance as well as independent fine and gross motor coordination skills.

Arguably the most important aspect of the rider's position is that it should be completely independent and supple. This is the foundation of good hand and body use, correct and effective communication and invisible aids. An independent seat stops riders from pulling or jerking on the reins for balance, thus protecting the horse's mouth. It prevents riders from giving two simultaneous but opposing messages which confuse horses.

Independent balance

Complete balance is essential for an independent seat. The average rider's balance develops automatically through riding mileage and will usually not need special attention. However, the process can be accelerated through appropriate body-use exercises because correct body use improves balance. Riders who are a little balance-challenged may need extra attention.

A balanced and independent seat is the only seat which allows clear communication with the horse. When balance reactions cause gripping with the legs, tightness in the waist, tension in the shoulders or balancing actions with the arms and hands, the use of these parts as aids of communication is neutralised. A consistent contact cannot develop and the painful pressure on the bars and tongue of the horse's mouth leads to defensive behaviour, often misinterpreted as 'resistance'.

This independent balance has to be developed to the point where riders do not need their hands, arms or legs to maintain balance on the horse and thus they have no need to pull involuntarily on the reins or grip with their legs, thereby giving opposing messages. The reins can, therefore, be used independently for the purpose for which they were designed – to transmit clear and accurate messages to the horse – and the legs can be used independently to transmit the leg aids to the horse.

Defining dynamic balance

Dynamic balance is balance on a moving object. It differs from static balance which is on a stationary object, usually the ground. Dynamic balance is more difficult to achieve than static balance, but it is the type necessary to become a good rider. During dynamic balance most of the muscles are constantly exercised as they contract and relax to adapt to the continuous change in the supporting surface (in this case, the horse). With every step the horse takes, the rider's body is moved by the horse. To compensate for this, the body adjusts itself automatically, and continuously, around its centre of gravity to stay in balance. Riders have to maintain this dynamic balance while simultaneously controlling a horse.

Developing and improving dynamic balance

The body's balance mechanism needs time to become familiar with the new sensations and movements of the support base. Through mileage and experience of the variety of equine movements and reactions, the body builds a memory of these movements. This leads to automatic anticipation of the horse's reactions and movements and speeds up the balance reactions. The discussion of the principles of developing dynamic balance, and the accompanying exercises that follow, are aimed mainly at helping beginner riders, and those who teach them.

1. Automatic protective balance reactions are fast. However, learning new dynamic balance develops from slow reactions to instantaneous reactions and should therefore be developed from slow movement of the support base (the horse) to fast movement of the support base. Therefore, beginner riders have to start at walk and, when the rider moves in balance at walk, progress can be made to a relatively slow/lazy trot. Beginner riders should not be expected to ride with significant impulsion – this can be increased progressively as balance and confidence improve. This procedure ensures that posture is maintained.

2. Balance and rhythm are interrelated in riders as well as in horses. When riders lose rhythm, they lose balance. When their balance is challenged, their rhythm changes. When the horse loses rhythm or balance, the rider also loses rhythm and balance. Because beginner riders are slow to react to changes of rhythm and direction, the trot should initially have an even rhythm to help both horse and rider maintain balance. Improve rhythm and balance by alternating short and long steps, first at the walk and then at the trot – as explained in Chapter 7.

3. Balance develops from a large base of support to a small base of support. The seat filling the saddle gives excellent support. Rising trot decreases the size of the base of support, thus challenging balance. Beginner riders thus flop back into the saddle. Gradual reductions in the base of support can be achieved in the following ways:
    - Alternate the size of the base of support by alternating standing and sitting in the stirrups, at walk.
    - Alternate the half-seat with posting at walk.
    - At trot, alternate rising, sitting, half-seat, forward seat and standing.

4. Balance develops from initially large reactions to eventual automatic invisible recruitment of the necessary muscle fibres. Beginner riders show large arm and crouching body balance reactions. As balance and familiarity develop, these movements become smaller and eventually disappear.

5. The human body becomes rigid in defence when there is a threat to its security. This rigidity will not disappear until the body feels safe again so, if this happens, it is first necessary to remove the perceived threat. For example, if a rider becomes unbalanced and tenses up at sitting trot, simply continuing in trot will increase rigidity and disturb balance so that the rider bounces even more. In such circumstances, the remedy is for the rider to correct this defensive rigidity as soon as it becomes apparent by immediately going back to walk and focusing on relaxing into the movement when starting at a slow trot again.

6. Balance is more stable when the centre of gravity is close to, and over the centre of, the support base. A slightly forward position in rising trot brings the centre of gravity in alignment with the base of support. It also lowers the centre of gravity. This position prevents the rider from getting behind the movement. The ear-shoulder-hip-heel alignment rule cannot apply to the rising trot because it places the rider behind the horse's movement. This causes inadequate balance and the rider cannot help but pull the horse in the mouth at every stride. At all times, during the rising trot, the rider's shoulders have to be slightly ahead of the hips to ensure good balance over their base of support (feet in stirrups).

below left Too upright a position in rising trot. The rider becomes behind the movement at every stride, bounces too high and pulls on the horse's mouth. The horse's topline muscles tighten.

below right The correct rising trot, with the rider's centre of gravity over her base of support, leading to good balance, staying with the movement and a soft contact.

7. Balance develops faster if the body is given the opportunity to learn automatically. Riders can teach their body to react and take over the balance function by taking their arms out of the balance reactions. If, instead, they hold onto the pommel of the saddle the holding arm does the balance work and the body does not learn to react and balance. The arms can be taken out of the equation in the following ways:
   • Pushing the knuckles down on the withers to ensure that the arms do not tighten to balance (see photo opposite).

- Resting the hands or fingers on the horse's withers or the pommel, rather than holding on.
- Riding with one hand down by the side.
- Relaxing the arms down by their sides and balancing with the body during lungeing.
- Doing asymmetrical flowing arm exercises while the horse is moving. For example, leaving the reins on the horse's neck and 'writing', with both hands, in space, or 'painting pictures', doing karate katas (dance-like movements) or 'directing an orchestra' until the jerky movements disappear.

A beginner in rising trot with fingers touching the withers to prevent arm balance reactions and teach the body to balance. Short-armed riders may have to lean forwards, but this is a temporary measure to correct balance and contact.

8. A supple body has faster reaction speed. Riders' 'waists' (the lumbar vertebrae) have to be especially supple to absorb the horse's movement in walk, sitting trot and canter. Riders can increase suppleness in this area by doing the following:
   - While maintaining the seat on the saddle, rotating the waist to the left and then to the right; 'drawing' a large circle on the saddle with the seat.
   - Adding speed to this rotation.
   - Alternately hollowing and rounding the back.
   - Alternately lifting one hip as high as possible with lifting the other hip by bending laterally in the waist.

9. Rotational exercises improve core muscle tone and speed up reactions. These include:
   - Touching the horse's right ear with the left hand and vice versa.
   - Turning and touching the horse's right rump with the left hand and vice versa.
   - Touching the right toe with the left hand and vice versa.
   - Placing hands on hips and rotating the body to both sides as far as it will go.

10. Challenging balance reactions gives the body 'experience'. In some of these exercises the rider will have to 'hold on' with the legs and in others they will re-arrange their body around its centre of gravity.
    - Rider leans their upper body to the side, but corrects their balance by re-arranging the body around its centre of gravity by bending at the waist and 'popping' their opposite hip out to the other side.
    - Rider leans over to one side as far as possible, then sits up and repeats the movement to the other side.
    - Rider leans backwards as far as possible without touching the horse.
    - Rider leans forwards, without changing body schema, to feel the back muscles tighten.
    - Rider leans forwards and pushes their backside out behind them as much as necessary to ensure that their centre of gravity is maintained over the base of support – the feet. This is the basis of a balanced jumping seat in which the body is balanced over the feet throughout the jump.

    Riders can do all these exercises with their arms by their sides and then with them stretched above their head, and notice the difference.

11. Conditioning muscles and improving their flexibility enhances overall muscle quality and assists balance reactions. Good muscle tone improves balance because it improves reaction time. The weaker the balance, the more

right When the rider bends in the waist the body rearranges around its centre of gravity.

far right Leaning over to challenge balance.

compensation and therefore energy and strength are required to maintain balance. Riders should therefore train to become fit, strong and supple.

12. Balance reactions are enhanced by progressing to changes of rhythm and speed. These can be accomplished by transitions from gait to gait and transitions within the gaits. Some examples are:
   - Walk to halt and back to walk.
   - Trot to walk and back to trot.
   - Riding fewer strides between the transitions.
   - Shortening and lengthening the walk strides.
   - Shortening and lengthening the trot strides.
   - Changing the speed of the walk every 10m.
   - Changing the speed of the trot every 10m.

13. Changing *direction* through school movements, initially with longer periods between the changes, also assists balance reactions. Following on with quicker changes of direction will further improve reaction speed.

above left Leaning forwards without changing the body schema. It is necessary to rest the hands on the horse's neck to prevent losing balance.

above right The balanced jumping seat with the centre of gravity over the base of support. (Note the difference between this position and that in the previous photo.) Riders can do all these exercises with their arms by their sides and then with them stretched above their head, and notice the difference.

INDEPENDENT COORDINATION

Effective communication with the horse is only possible with a well-coordinated body and independent use of the limbs.

Our bodies naturally work in coordinated systems in patterns of movement to produce poised movement. (A clear example of a pattern of movement is a gymnast or high board diver's intricate tumble. Imagine the difficulty for the body in learning and establishing such a pattern.) This means that movement in one part normally has a significant effect on movement in other parts of the body. This has two implications for riders.

- The horse's specific biomechanical structure gives him limited ability to form new patterns of movement. This means that riders can control and manoeuvre the horse's entire neuro-muscular system (including the automatic reactions) by influencing only the four key points of control as described in Chapters 1 and 2.

- For the rider this means that normally, turning the head or looking down, can change the entire body posture and therefore give the horse mixed messages. However, humans can learn endless new patterns of movement.

Independent coordination means that riders have to learn new coordinated patterns of movement for communicating with the horse without the danger of mixed messages. In these new patterns each limb or body part should be able to do a different task without the movement affecting the coordination of any other limb or body part. This means that the seat and each limb can apply individual aids independently without causing involuntary 'associated' movements (see next section) in other body parts, and so these aids thus do not disturb the rest of the body's coordination, balance and rhythm. The new pattern thus ensures that turning the head will not lead to the shoulders or hips turning; looking down will not cause rounded shoulders; vibrating the fingers will not tighten the arms. Once learnt, the body never forgets the new pattern.

It is difficult to change a postural habit (movement pattern) and to learn a new one in riding. The old pattern is an ingrained movement memory and, when a stressful situation occurs or your concentration is disturbed, your body will want to revert to the original pattern.

Young riders learn new movement patterns with great ease because their brains develop new nerve pathways. After approximately the age of 25 the brain apparently does not develop new pathways – it relies on existing pathways and has to take detours to reach the final destination. Therefore, older riders take longer to learn the new coordination skills of advanced riding techniques.

The new corrected pattern or position may initially feel uncomfortable and wrong, but with repetition it becomes effective and easy. An example of this is the difficulty in maintaining an inside bend with the inside leg in half-pass while the outside leg pushes the horse over. It feels most uncomfortable initially, but after enough practice, becomes automatic.

Some postural patterns of movement are temporary while learning a new skill. They are caused by inadequate coordination, balance or strength. Changing these prematurely may be detrimental to rider effectiveness. They should thus largely be ignored until the rider has developed the required physical skill to enable him or her to control the horse as well as performing the movement. For example, some riders do not have adequate coordination, timing, skill or strength* in their leg adductors (lateral pushing muscles) to convince the horse to move off light pressure. These riders may feel the need to lean their bodies to the side. Placing weight behind the pushing leg gives more effectiveness to it in leg-yield, shoulder-in and half-pass. It also reinforces the feel in the muscles. (Compare this to pushing a spade into hard ground. Your weight, placed on your foot on the spade, creates more pressure). However, this is a temporary measure until riders are able to co-ordinate the use of all the muscles needed for these actions. When their adductor and abdominal oblique muscles become strong and effective, their timing, co-ordination and technique improve. This is also improved when the horse learns to move off light pressure. (I personally like the rider to go through this process of pushing because it highlights body awareness and coordination when learning new movement patterns. When riders do this they also learn faster to ride effectively.)

Note When learning lateral movements on a horse not trained in the movement, a certain amount of strength is required to give strong pressure if the horse does not react to light pressure – see Chapter 7.

Inadequate coordination affects rider technique: it causes rigidity and thus slow, contorted movements; it blocks the fine-tuning needed for exact invisible rider-horse communication and is a main cause of horses receiving mixed messages. It is thus essential for riders to learn riding-specific coordination systems to become a 'riding one-man-band' – perfect multi-taskers. To get some idea of what is required, try this exercise: play the children's game of circling your one hand on your head while you tap your stomach with your other hand. Add to this hopping on one leg and finally add kicking the other leg in and out. This is the type of independent coordination necessary in order to communicate effectively with the horse.

MAC DID EXCELLENT shoulder-in at walk on the left rein, but on the right rein he seemed to try to avoid it and would 'freeze' or piaffe instead. We assumed that the right shoulder-in problem was caused by physical discomfort. I rode the shoulder-in on Mac to diagnose the cause. To my surprise, the horse did the exercise with ease. The cause was the rider, who was blocking the movement through inadequate independent coordination. The harder she tried to use her leg, the more she pulled with her arms. By observing my technique, she realised that there should be no pulling, but very light contact. After Sarah corrected her coordination, Mac did the shoulder-in with ease.

An independent seat needs superior gross and fine motor coordination skills. Unfortunately this is neglected in many riding programmes. Independent coordination cannot be learnt by sitting still or doing nothing; it can only be learnt through movement. This means that form follows function.

Associated movements

The extraneous associated or 'parasitic' movements that I've previously mentioned in passing appear automatically when learning complex physical skills. They are commonly seen in the development of young children. For example, when doing a difficult task with one hand, the other hand may, inadvertently, mimic the movements. When using scissors, the child's other hand or tongue may move as they 'help' to cut.

These associated or parasitic movements have to be inhibited to ensure poised athletic movement. In riding, the seat can only become independent when the rider can isolate certain muscle groups to use them as effective tools of communication, without associated movements creeping in. The rider's arms, hands, legs and seat can then all perform independent skilled activities without affecting each other. The whole body, without affecting these skilled movements, also has to be able to maintain balance independently.

Most beginner and novice riders do not have independent body use and cannot separate the movements of their individual limbs. This interferes with rider-horse communication, especially with rein aids, but is also very common with leg aids when learning lateral movements. The associated movements when using the non-dominant (most commonly left) leg are usually more problematic than in the dominant (most commonly right) leg. The dominant leg tends to 'assist' when the non-dominant is pushing. For example while performing a turn on the forehand, riders find it difficult to separate the action of their two legs. They are often not able to push laterally with one leg alone: the 'passive' leg automatically joins in and gives the horse two conflicting messages. The same problem occurs when riding the leg-yield and the shoulder-in.

A major part of learning a new pattern of movement in any sport is to dispose of associated movements. For example, riders first have to learn to do 'nothing' with the non-active leg. Only then can it become passive or learn to do a different activity. Riders also have to learn to coordinate new patterns of movement without associated movements. This may initially cause a little rigidity and tension, but as independent coordination develops, so the associated movements disappear. The fastest method of learning and correcting coordination in riding is through learning lateral movements correctly.

Gross motor coordination

Gross motor coordination (GMC) is the coordination of large body movements. This includes leg and arm movements. Correct leg aids are dependent on good GMC and therefore riders have to do specific exercises to learn independent limb use. Most exercise techniques such as Pilates, yoga and gym exercises improve gross motor coordination. However, the most effective exercises for riders are those specific to riding, especially the asymmetrical leg and arm exercises. The best exercises are the actual lateral movements of turn on the forehand, leg-yield, shoulder-in and half-pass because, through doing these, riders learn riding-specific patterns of movement. It is essential though, that they are executed correctly without undesirable associated movements creeping in.

MY FIRST ATTEMPTS AT shoulder-in were completely unsuccessful. I attended a riding course with a top American trainer of the time. Unfortunately my Thoroughbred was in such a heightened state of fright/flight that my uncoordinated attempts proved useless. Of course I blamed the horse. Our second attempt was guided by a trainer who tried to teach us shoulder-in on a circle but, without it being preceded by learning to leg-yield, it set us up for failure. She exclaimed that the horse was not ready and left it at that. I then tried to learn it from a book. My poor coordination led to neck bend without much angle but, in my ignorance, I thought I had it. After more frustrating and unsuccessful attempts in which I blamed the horse for not 'wanting to do it', we finally got it. I initially assumed it was the horse who had got it, but then realised that the horse could now do it because my body coordination had finally developed to the extent whereby I was not giving him opposing messages.

Fine motor coordination

Fine motor coordination (FMC) is the coordination of the hands and, especially the fingers. Good FMC ensures that riders can influence their horses correctly through the reins. We use a variety of fine hand and finger movements for meaningful communications with the horse. Minimum effort, invisible communication through the bit using fine, soft finger vibrations, light elastic contact and correct timing and technique are the all-important end products of good FMC.

Many mouth problems have been caused by riders' inadequate FMC skills. The only method of correcting such mouth problems is by allowing self-carriage via a yielding contact. This is done through pressure-release finger and hand actions but, without good FMC, this is not possible. Of course, riders cannot be expected to start with the end product of invisible aids (as is often expected). However, it is important that they start learning the FMC skills of correct hand use from the outset of learning to ride, in order to protect horses' mouths.

FMC has to be independent from other body movements such as balance reactions and associated movements. Generally, the hands and arms work as a unit: movement in one affects the other. The muscles responsible for the fingers 'sponging' the reins are all located in the forearms and thus affect the whole arm, often causing elbow rigidity. Riders have to learn to use independent finger vibrations which do not cause tightening or co-contraction in their elbows and shoulders. The elbows and shoulders have to learn to relax when the fingers vibrate or sponge the reins. This is similar to playing a musical instrument.

The hand and wrist muscles are situated in the forearms.

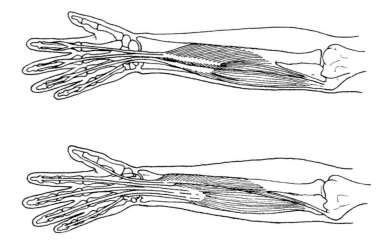

Riders who have not developed sufficient feel, timing and coordination move their hands and elbows quite visibly. As FMC develops, feel and timing improve. When riders' hands and arms are independent from balance reactions and associated movements and have independent and correct coordination, they *appear to be* still.

Developing fine motor coordination

Below are the requirements for developing fine motor coordination, together with some exercises that will help achieve this.

1. **Limbs devoid of tension.** Tension and anxiety work against the development of coordination. With rigidity, movements slow down and become larger. Imagine catching a ball with tight arms. Rigid bodies and movements cannot communicate independently or with the correct timing. Inadequately coordinated, clumsy instructions with extraneous movements confuse horses and cause

anxiety, leading to over-reactions and poor execution from the horse, such as loss of rhythm, loss of balance and turning too suddenly. They often lead also to defensive mouth behaviour: 'Only the rider who is free from contraction will have a horse equally free from contraction'.[9] The ability to relax the antagonists while the movers do the action allows for a fast reaction speed and thus correct timing of the aids.*

In order to reduce tension in your posture, try the following:

- Relax and stretch your abdominal, hip and pectoral muscles to allow an upright posture.
- Learn to push out your stomach by pushing your diaphragm out. Push your belly button forwards without hollowing your back.
- Relax your face. This tends to relax your whole body.
- Relax your arms by resting your little fingers on the horse's withers.

2. **Well-developed core muscles.** The core is generally defined as the torso muscles, which provide stability of the trunk over the pelvis. This is needed to generate power and mobility to the limbs, thus assisting independent limb use. The following will help develop these muscles:

- Push out your stomach by tightening your diaphragm as in the second point above.
- Tighten your rhomboid group of muscles between the tips of your shoulder blades by imagining an angel pulling its wingtips together as explained later in Chapter 7. Stretch your body up. This contracts your multifidus muscles around your spine* (see note below). Do abdominal muscle exercises such as rotations, side-bending and sit-ups.

3. **Fast reaction speed.** If you are too slow, the horse will get the message too late and your late release of pressure will reward the incorrect action.

- Start by improving body awareness as explained in Chapter 5.
- Improve feel as explained in Chapter 5. Learn to differentiate between the pressures your horse produces on your body. Once you feel changes faster, your reaction speed should increase.

4. **Agility.** This helps with all sport, but even a less-agile rider can develop sufficient coordination to ride well.

*Note The movers are the muscles producing the action. The antagonists are the opposing muscles which have to relax to allow controlled smooth movement.

*Note The rhomboid muscles lie between the shoulder blades and pull them closer together (see illustration on page 141). The multifidus muscles criss-cross the entire spinal column. They stretch the vertebral column, rotate it and bend it laterally.

Further development of rider coordination

It is not possible to learn fine motor coordination simply by holding the hands still. If the hands do nothing, they will never learn the fine motor skills needed for invisible communication. Imagine learning to touch type without moving all your fingers.

Let us use learning the piano and learning a new dressage movement as examples of how coordination develops. Both gross and fine motor coordination develop from:

1. **Slow movements to fast movements.** The novice musician plays 'Twinkle twinkle little star' with slow-moving fingers, progresses to playing it faster and can finally play a Mozart concerto with fast-moving fingers. In a similar way, novice rider's timing of the pressure-release aids is slow and thus late and at the wrong moment, however the rider starts to learn the shoulder-in at walk, progresses to trot and can finally do it at canter.

2. **Large movements to small movements.** The beginner musician uses large finger movements to play 'Twinkle twinkle little star', then progresses to smaller finger movements and can finally play a Mozart concerto with small coordinated finger movements. Beginner riders use large, clumsy, slow and ineffective arm movements, and large and slow kicks when learning to coordinate the aids. Riders' hand and finger coordination then develops from whole-arm pulling, nagging and sawing, with large and slow rein squeezes and vibrations, to delicate feather-like movements with individual fingers. When well coordinated, these movements become invisible.

5. **Simple movement patterns to complex movement patterns.** The novice pianist learns to play the tune with the right hand, then increases the complexity by adding the left hand to play different notes with each hand. Finally the musician can play a complicated concerto with fast and delicate finger movements together with use of the foot pedals. Beginner riders cannot multi-task. Movement in one part affects other parts when learning to coordinate the aids. These clumsy movements finally develop into complex movements such as half-pass and pirouette, with all four limbs multi-tasking. Riders eventually learn to react fast enough to ride the horse in balance 'between hand and leg' with only small finger movements and light leg aids. Thus, from the highly visible to the invisible.

The good news is that all riders possess the ability to develop adequate FMC skills to eventually ride with invisible aids. (Advanced riders sometimes use larger movements when training young horses or when retraining horses with problematic rein contact, but their timing is exquisite.)

Ambidexterity and coordination

Horses should ideally become 'ambidextrous', or as near to that as possible, so correct training should result in equal muscle development, reaction and suppleness on both sides of the horse's body. Riders have to match this to ensure that the horse receives equal bilateral instructions. In general, however, the human body is not ambidextrous, so riders' aids are not the same on each side of the horse. Apart from the left-handed minority, most riders have a weaker and less coordinated left side. In general, right-dominant riders habitually pull with their left arms and yield with their right arms. The opposite applies to left-dominant riders. It is our duty, as riders, to develop our balance, strength and especially coordination equally on both sides, so the weaker arm, hand and leg should be exercised independently to develop equal bilateral coordination, suppleness and strength.

Here is an exercise to test your riding ambidexterity. As you are sitting on the saddle, turn your hips in a circle to the right. Now turn them to the left. If you cannot do it equally well in both directions, you are not ambidextrous enough and your horse will not do the movements equally on both sides.

The pulling left hand and arm syndrome

The phenomenon of the pulling left hand/arm is one of the most common examples of one-sidedness in riders. It highlights how inadequate coordination causes associated movements because the cause is not in the arm, but in the rider's weaker and less coordinated non-dominant leg, usually the left. It is most commonly seen in the shoulder-in and the inside bend on the rider's weaker side. The inside leg has to push the horse's ribcage to maintain the slight inside bend. The inside hand has to vibrate the reins to ask the horse to bend (and release when he reacts correctly), but must not pull. However, the non-dominant leg is ineffective at moving the horse over or pushing the ribcage, so the inside (left) hand and arm unintentionally try to 'assist' or mimic it by pulling on the rein. This gives an incorrect opposing aid, blocks forward movement and invokes a pulling response from the horse. When riders are instructed to yield this arm, the leg also stops 'working'. In left-dominant people the opposite applies – see photos overleaf.

FIONA WAS CONSTANTLY pulling on the right rein although she was right-handed. It transpired that her dominance had been changed during childhood (this was the fashion at the time). Although her right hand had become dominant, her right leg remained non-dominant, less coordinated and weaker. It turned her right hand into the pulling 'helper'.

right The pulling left arm is causing the rider's right arm to give and the body to twist to the left; it is pullling the horse's head into a false bend – see also page 54.

below Another view of the pulling left arm syndrome ... and the pulling left arm corrected, leading to less neck bend in shoulder-in.

Exercises to improve strength and coordination of the non-dominant side

The coordination of the non-dominant hand, arm and leg can only improve if riders practise and develop coordination and strength off the horse.

Gross motor coordination exercises

1. Tie a strong elastic band around a pole. Place your weak leg inside it and pull the band towards your other leg, strengthening your adductor muscles.

2. Move a brick or ground pole with your weak leg, pushing it sideways.

3. 'Move' a cupboard with the foot of your weak leg.

4. Ask your gym instructor to work out a programme for individual leg adductor strengthening.

5. Set your body up to dispose of the associated movement automatically. Use two-handed techniques in leg-yield and shoulder-in. This prevents too much bend on the inside rein, especially on your weak side. Leg-yield with your weak leg on the inside.
   - Intertwine your thumbs, hold a thumb or touch your knuckles together to prevent your weak arm from pulling.
   - Push the knuckles of your weak hand into the horse's withers to prevent it from inadvertently pulling.
   - Place an elastic band around your wrists (not so tight that it prevents hand movement). This prevents your weak arm from pulling and fixes the problem

Holding a thumb to prevent the left arm from pulling in shoulder-in.

above left An elastic band applied around the wrists sets the body up to learn subconsciously. It learns fast when its choice is limited.

above right The band has been removed. The rider can now squeeze the rein without pulling the arm back or twisting her body.

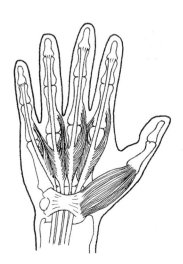

The intrinsic muscles of the hands.

instantly. It relaxes your elbows and upper arms, allowing them to move with the horse's mouth. It renders both arms out of action and forces your fingers to do the work. Your legs immediately become more effective and proactive.

Fine motor coordination exercises

Homework exercises include writing, playing the piano, guitar and typing with the non-dominant hand and fingers. Pouring drinks, turning on taps and brushing teeth are all activities which can improve fine motor coordination of the non-dominant hand. Other ideas are:

1. Touch your thumb with each individual finger. Start with the index finger and follow on to the little finger. Then reverse the action, starting at the little finger. Start slowly and increase the speed so that it equals that of your dominant hand.

2. Keep your fingers straight while you open and close each one individually sideways. Strengthening these intrinsic muscles helps to prevent the reins from slipping.

Start these exercises with both hands simultaneously as this is easier. Follow on by exercising the weak hand separately. Become aware of the difference in quality. Do these exercises with the wrist in extension, mid-position and in flexion. This demonstrates the difference in ease of fine finger movements in the different wrist positions and how it affects communication with the horse.

Chapter 4

||||||||||||||||||||||||||||||||||||||||||||||||||||||||||||||||||||||||||||||||||||||||||||||||||||||||||||||||||||||||||||||||||||||||

BODY LANGUAGE

THE BODY LANGUAGE we use to communicate with the horse is a language of feel. The horse feels the explanations (aids) and the rider feels the response from the horse. It is similar to the communication of deaf-blind people. Helen Keller, who was born deaf and blind, learnt to feel the words spelled out on her hands, and to feel the speaker's vocal cords with her hands. When the rider explains to the horse what he has to do with his head, he feels these 'words' through the bit. He feels through his sides and his back the 'words' telling him what to do with his body and his legs. In turn, the rider feels the horse's response through their body, hands and legs.

FEEL

'Feel' is the ability not simply to feel but also to analyse automatically, in the finest detail, every influence the horse has on your body. It also encompasses the ability to transmit signals to the horse in an empathetic way. It is a prerequisite for the development of the art of riding and incorporates four different skills:

1. Feel perception.

2. Anticipation – perceiving the signals and thereby anticipating the change.

3. Timing (reaction speed).

4. The technique of passing the message to the horse.

Feel as a gift

The 'art' of dressage is in the feel; it is the essence for which every rider strives. This element divides the great from the not-so-great. Natural feel, in riders, can be compared to perfect pitch in musicians. Only the Mozarts of the world have it. These riders are the lucky tiny minority who have been born with this gift. The other 99 per cent of the riding population have to develop it.

We are all born with differing abilities to perceive and react. Riders can be categorised into four groups in terms of this ability.

1. Those born with the gift of perfect natural feel. These riders do not have to think about what they are feeling or doing; it is automatic. They are the few who have become the great equestrians of their time – names such as de la Guérinière, Baucher, L'Hotte, Oliveira, Klimke and a few others. However, more than this gift alone is necessary in order to become great.

2. A second group of riders with excellent feel are those with lightning-fast tactile and kinaesthetic perception and reaction speed. These riders usually have a background of success in various other sports such as swimming, athletics or gymnastics. They, too, have the ability to become top riders.

3. The majority of riders have normal levels of feel, but their analysis of what it conveys is slow. These riders *can* ride at a high level, but have to hone and develop feel. They need exceptional motivation, discipline and practice.

4. A small group possess inadequate feel, but even they can develop and improve this ability. These are the slow learners who lack talent. They move from frustrated trainer to frustrated trainer in their attempt to become better riders. They, too, can learn to ride at a high level provided they find a teacher who is able to 'diagnose' and teach feel.

In search of feel

Let us investigate the elusive quality of feel. Through evolution, mankind's sense of feel has slowly become inhibited. We have become largely dependent on our visual and auditory senses and perceptions to learn and to communicate. Learning to ride does involve these fields of perception to a certain degree, but the art of riding is far more dependent on good feel.

Feel comprises the development and perceptual use of two senses – the tactile sense and the kinaesthetic sense. These two senses have to be developed to their utmost if riders want to attain greatness.

The tactile sense

The human tactile sense consists of three elements:

1. **Heat perception.** Awareness of heat and cold is not generally applicable to training horses, but it does assist in finding areas of injury. People with well-developed heat perception can feel heat radiating from inflamed areas on the horse without touching him.

2. **Light touch.** A doctor will test this with a wad of cotton wool. The nerves, which are stimulated by light touch, are situated in the superficial layers of the skin. The sensation of light touch reaches the brain faster than that of deep pressure. This is the reason why we react quickly to a bothersome fly. Light touch, a tickle, is mainly used to reward the horse because the feedback is immediate.

3. **Deep pressure.** Light touch and deep pressure differ neurologically. The nerve endings for deep pressure are situated in the deeper layers of the skin, and involve structures such as muscles, below the skin. Deep pressure sensation is crucial for the development of feel. It is the sense we use to communicate and explain our wishes to the horse. This is the two-way body language. This pressure-release language is dependent on the deep pressure sensation of both horse and rider.

   The deep pressure receptors are sensitive to *changes* in pressure. Animals do not feel pressure as such; they feel changes of pressure: 'Large changes of pressure result in large responses, but only during the change.'[1] Perception of consistent pressure diminishes and disappears after about thirty seconds, which is why all aids should be given in a pressure-release manner. Horses' mouths become ever more insensitive when riders constantly pull, hang, or the bit does not move for more than thirty seconds. This also applies to constant leg pressure because they habituate to the pressure. So their riders gradually take a stronger contact and use stronger leg aids.

   Our weight aids are based mainly on deep pressure perception in the horse, not on touch sensation. This is the reason why the thickness of a saddle does not make a significant difference to the horse's perception of pressure. It is also the reason why riders can feel through gloves.

The kinaesthetic and proprioceptive senses

These senses perceive:

1. The position of each body part, wherever it is, constantly.

2. The speed of movement.

3. The amount of muscular tension (pull on the muscles).

4. The distance one part of the body is from another.

Coordination, balance, the feeling of the horse pulling, lifting his head, leaning his shoulder, collecting and the angle of shoulder-in, for example, are all dependent on kinaesthetic sensations. All the horse's movements move a part of the rider's body. The sensory organs in the rider's skin, ears, muscles and joints perceive changes in the body. The brain perceives these messages, integrates them and transforms them into messages of muscular action, instructing the muscles to react appropriately. The body and mind become inseparable during physical activity. The gifted rider with lightning-fast perception of sensations and feel reacts automatically to these sensations.

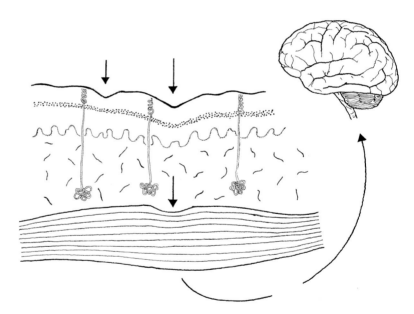

Sensations on the skin. The top arrows show light touch and the arrows through to the muscles show deep pressure on the skin. The nerve impulses move to the brain, which turns the sensation into perception.

Each person has their preferred perceptual system of learning. Some learn best through visual perception (demonstration) while others learn better through auditory perception (verbal instructions). Riders with good feel rely largely on their outstanding tactile and kinaesthetic perceptual abilities. They learn through doing. To become a great rider, you have to become increasingly aware of your kinaesthetic and tactile perceptions and learn to change your primary dependence from visual and auditory perception to kinaesthetic and tactile perception. Learning a physical skill, such as the art of riding, is slowest if done through auditory perception. Fortunately, we can all improve all our perceptual abilities.

The horse, too, learns the rider's body language through touch, deep pressure (weight changes), proprioception (limb placement) and kinaesthesia (movement).

Tension and emotions such as anxiety, frustration and impatience, block feel because the brain is distracted in defence mode and the body becomes rigid and less reactive to feel sensations. Relaxation thus improves feel.

Anticipation

Riders with well-developed feel have effective control. They feel *before* the mistake or resistance appears. However, they also need the correct technique and good timing to intervene and ensure that the correct movement will be executed or the incorrect one eliminated. This pre-empting is part of what the great écuyer, General L'Hotte, referred to as 'equestrian tact'. He said, 'Progress will be all the more timely when the rider, forewarned by his equestrian tact, will be able to forestall a false movement by modifying the contractions which give the position which is its precursor.'[2] This is when horse and rider appear to be in true harmony; when the rider appears to do nothing. The control is mild because the rider corrects the mistakes before they have materialised. The aids are thus invisible. Most of good riding is about preventing loss of balance, preventing loss of focus and preventing incorrect reactions. The majority of riders, however, have to go through a fairly long process of learning feel before they can anticipate the horse's actions and prevent the horse from responding incorrectly.

All riders should learn to sense the nuances and react instantly to pre-empt the horse before:

- Loss of balance (the contact becomes stronger, the bend starts to change).

- Loss of rhythm (feel the first step of the rhythm change).

- Loss or change of bend (the rein pressure starts to swap).

- Contact changes (the rein pressure starts to change on your ring finger).

- The horse hollows (the contact becomes stronger).

- The horse goes onto the forehand (the contact becomes stronger, the rider's upper body starts to rock forwards and the hindquarters feel higher than the shoulders).

- An incorrect canter depart (horse's weight is on the wrong leg, his bend is incorrect and his wrong shoulder is in a forward position. The rider's wrong hip and leg are in a forward position).

This pre-empting eradicates most of the resistances encountered when training horses.

When this advanced feel has developed, riders use minute finger movements for maintaining the inside bend, for half-halts and to prevent the horse from using his neck for balance. Their leg aids are light because they can anticipate before the horse loses his bend, lateral steps or impulsion.

Horses react to movement, and changes in their environment. They will lift their heads to see, spook at or shy away from a new or changed object in their visual field. An important part of anticipation for the rider is to be vigilant of your surroundings. Assess the surrounding area by becoming aware of everything in your visual field. Learn to recognise the elements to which horses generally respond and the manner in which they respond. Once the distractions are recognised you can anticipate them and intervene. This helps you to prevent the shoulder from 'falling' in or out towards the stable or other horses when riding a circle and to prevent the head lifting and back hollowing when the horse seeks to look up or to shy.

Horses' reactions often show repetitive behaviour. They spook at the same rocks and logs every time they hack out. They are distracted and consistently repeat the same behaviour at the same spot in the arena. This behaviour is usually triggered initially by something or some movement a horse sees/wants to look at coming into or passing his visual field. The movement of the horse's eyes causes movement of his head and trunk* (see note opposite). When his eyes look up, his head moves up and his neck and back hollow. His ears generally also point in the same direction as the object he is looking at. His repetitive reactions and distractions become predictable after one or two circuits of the arena. This assists both trainer and rider, especially when the rider is learning to ride and to simultaneously

below left The horse pricks his ears and starts to lift his head as he is distracted.

below right The horse lifts his head higher because the rider has not prevented it.

The horse's ears show his distraction, but the rider's timely intervention prevents the head from lifting.

Note The small muscles interconnecting the occipital bone, the atlas and the axis (the skull and neck vertebrae) contract when the horse moves his eyes. Place your fingers over the small muscles connecting your skull to your neck (at the base of your skull). Close your eyes and move them from side to side, up and down. You will feel movement in these muscles.

maintain a round flexor frame. This reaction can be prevented by asking the horse to keep looking down.

The horse will also be likely to soften and yield to the bit every time he gets to the same spot. Riders should learn to anticipate when a horse will yield with ease. These moments in the correct flexor frame can then be lengthened by preventing the head lift.

Horses also lose rhythm at the same spot on a circle repeatedly. They may speed up as they turn to face home or slow down when they move away from the arena entrance, or when passing other horses. They often break the canter at the same spot each time, which riders should also learn to recognise and pre-empt.

I WAS SCHOOLING A young pony in the sunshine for a few consecutive days. He was completely accepting of the barrels outside the arena. However, after a downpour he refused to go near the barrels. At first I could not understand his reluctance, but then realised that the wet barrels now had a slight shimmer. The difference turned them into completely new objects for the horse. He soon relaxed when I introduced him to the barrels as though they were new objects.

Riders often become frustrated when a horse spooks at an object which he has seen before. To avoid this frustration they need to learn to perceive as horses do so that they can anticipate the horse's reactions and prevent them.

Timing

The art of communication in riding is also dependent on timing (in fact, micro-timing) and technique (which we'll discuss shortly). These are the other elements of what L'Hotte called 'equestrian tact': 'One ingredient that each and every method needs in order to succeed is 'equestrian tact', that is, 'perfect timing and good measure.'[3]

Inadequate timing of the aids is probably the biggest obstacle in the development of the art of riding. Timing is dependent on feel because changes in the horse should be perceived instantly. The effect, whether positive or negative, should be analysed automatically and the appropriate reaction should be made – all with split-second timing. This ability, together with perfect neuro-muscular reaction speed, is what differentiates the gifted from the ordinary rider. This is because it is relatively easy to master good technique, but good timing can take many years to develop. Riding is all about feeling and reacting, not about waiting and thinking, or the golden moment will be lost.

Perfect timing is essential to ensure that the horse is prepared for and understands each movement, and thus to prevent undesirable balance reactions. Riders have to learn to pre-empt the horse and intervene with split-second timing before the horse can act to evade, resist, make a mistake, lift his head, hollow, or lose rhythm, balance, focus and bend. This takes experience, knowledge of equine behaviour, and feel.

Most riders *do* feel the changes in the horse's attitude or movement, but many register the change too slowly. Thus their reactions and corrections are too late, missing the psychological and physical moment for the aid. This makes a significant difference to the correctness of a movement. Learning is thus slow for both horse and rider.

If the rider's timing of the aids ('explanations') is out by a second, the horse will:

- Not connect the response to the stimulus and thus not learn. If the reward is too late after the action, the horse will not be able to make the connection. So, too, with punishment.

- Not react as required. For example, if the aid for walk to canter is late by a split second the horse's weight will be on the incorrect leg and his legs will be in the wrong phase of the stride pattern to take the correct lead. He will thus shuffle into the canter.

- Be rewarded for incorrect behaviour.

PIPPIN BOXED without difficulty until someone put too much pressure on her. This made the pony rear. The handler released the rein pressure as Pippin reared. The incorrect timing of this action, after the pony had started to rear, rewarded her for rearing. She thus learnt that pressure on the lead rein meant rearing. (The correct method is to prevent the rear by not pressurising the horse to the point of rearing and by feeling the first signs and instantly bending the horse.)

- Lose balance and the round flexor frame if the half-halt is too late.

- 'Fall in' (lose the bend and change his weight) on turns if the rider does not prevent it in good time.

Feel has to be developed to perfect timing, but this can be a complex process. Only by the rider getting the timing right will the horse react correctly and reinforce the correct feel and timing for the rider. This applies to timing of the aids as well as timing to prevent unwanted reactions such as snatching the reins.

Timing is affected by factors such as tiredness, stress, PMS, tension and anxiety. Under these conditions, the rider's timing will be too slow because muscle tension slows down reaction speed. Consequently the horse does not perform well and usually takes the blame.

Beginner riders' coordination is too slow, their reactions are too late and their actions too prolonged. Their reins slip or are too long for direct and timely communication with the horse. As feel develops, reaction time speeds up. Through a little anticipation, the timing becomes faster, the aids lighter and mistakes are prevented. Both timing and feel improve steadily over the course of time.

Here is an exercise to show the differences between correct and incorrect timing. Balance a chair on its back legs. Find the point where you can maintain the balance with tiny finger movements. This demonstrates how small your finger movements should be to maintain the horse's balance or steady contact when your timing is correct. Notice how the chair falls when the movements become too large, too small and ineffective, or the timing is too slow. These result in large corrective actions.

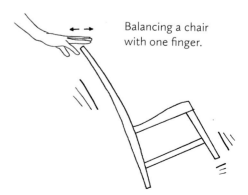

Balancing a chair with one finger.

Personality type and reaction time

A rider's personality type significantly affects reaction speed. In terms of feel in riding, two personality traits need consideration: the thinkers/planners and the reactors. The former almost always have their pressure-release out of sync with the horse's yielding. Their reaction speed is too slow to correct the horse; they tend to react long after the horse has produced incorrect behaviour. They apply pressure too late and release the pressure well after the horse has yielded. The late reaction rewards the wrong movement. It 'teaches' horses incorrect responses. These are the riders who are the most difficult to teach and who tend to learn the slowest. However, with determination and self-discipline, they too can become good riders.

ALIDE, A TYPICAL 'thinker/planner', could not maintain a steady head-carriage in her horse. Her anticipation, timing and reactions were too slow to prevent the slight head lift; she was closing her fingers after the horse had lifted his nose.

Dismounted exercises, with me acting as the horse (as described in Chapter 5), were done to speed up her reaction time. She had to react immediately by squeezing the rein between us as she felt the pressure increase on her fingers. Halfway through the exercise she simply stopped reacting – her mind had drifted.

Technique

Technique is all about learning gross and fine motor coordination. Learning the correct technique of body, leg, hand and finger use for invisible aids is an important ingredient of successful communication. The coordination of the different techniques is fairly easy to learn, provided they are taught correctly. The old patterns of movement and old postural habits have to be eradicated and replaced with new patterns. Riders have to learn to multi-task. This all takes practice. The four steps described in Chapter 7 encompass most of the techniques needed to elicit the correct reactions from the horse.

Mistakes of timing and technique are often seen in flying changes. Flying changes are not difficult for horses, but riders generally have difficulty when learning the technique and timing. Clean changes are dependent on perfect rider timing. If the aid is a split second too late, the horse's legs are in the incorrect position to execute a clean change.

SARAH HAD DIFFICULTY in perfecting her flying changes. Her technique was observed and analysed.

1. Her initial mistake was to turn her shoulders instead of her hips. This made her new outside hand move forwards, thus losing control of the horse's out-

side shoulder and losing the bend. The horse's weight stayed on his inside shoulder. He thus could not change legs.

2. She leaned forwards in the habitual foetal crouch commonly seen when riders learn new techniques. This meant that her seat was out of the saddle and ineffective.

3. She used her inside leg inadvertently together with her outside leg. These two opposing messages confused the horse.

4. She could not yield her arms into the change stride. This prevented the horse from taking a longer stride with more air time for a clean change.

5. She had the habit of looking down to see whether the horse had changed leads. Her seat thus lifted from the saddle.

After doing three clean changes across the diagonal she made the comment that it had become really easy once she had learnt to feel and could use her body correctly with the correct timing.

Incorrectly schooled horses who have developed defences to bit pressure complicate the development of good timing and technique.

NON-VERBAL BODY LANGUAGE

Horses learn fastest through two techniques: facilitation of automatic reactions together with conditioning.

Facilitation of automatic reactions

'Almost all the practices which aim at the submission of a horse have their point of departure in the animal's instincts …. Nature is the most important teacher. Its book is the most accurate, the wisest, and the most useful one can consult.'[4]

The fastest method of training horses is through the non-verbal communication techniques of 'facilitation of movement' together with conditioning. Facilitation of movement uses the horse's automatic balance and neck reactions and patterns of movement as explained in Chapter 2. We manoeuvre the horse into a position which will automatically elicit the correct balance reaction, movement pattern or ENR to produce the correct response. This ensures that the horse will react correctly the first time he is asked to do a specific movement. An example of this is the canter depart:

1. Position the horse so that his inside shoulder is ahead of his outside shoulder and his weight-bearing is on his outside fore and hind leg.

2. Push his ribcage with your inside leg.

3. Ask him to yield slightly to your inside rein by bending his own neck (no pulling to the inside).

4. Hold the outside rein to prevent him from changing his weight to his inside forelimb.

5. Keep your outside leg back to prevent him from moving his hindquarters out and change his weight to his inside hind leg.

These actions, plus intent and correct timimg should elicit a correct depart.

Conditioning – the pressure-release system

Horses cannot see all the rider's actions on their backs. They can hear and learn to understand single words and perhaps simple phrases, but not detailed verbal instructions. Besides, outside stimuli are not permitted in competition dressage. Xenophon said, 'The horse, it is obvious, is not open to instruction by speech and reasoning.'[5] They also cannot second-guess our often clumsy, vague and meaningless communications, although riders often expect this to happen. However, they can *feel* every movement the rider makes. The most reliable sensory organs to use for communicating with the horse are thus those of the tactile senses. Horses dislike pressure. A pressure-release system is thus the ideal training tool.

The aids we use to influence our horses are based on pressure and the timely release of pressure. Horses have to learn to yield to this pressure. Riders have to learn to release the pressure at precisely the correct moment.

This pressure-release system of communicating with horses is one of the oldest methods of aiding and training horses: it has been advocated by all the top trainers from Xenophon around 350 BC to the present. However, despite being the basis of training horses for many centuries, it seems to be widely misunderstood. The principle is that we ask the horse to yield to light pressure and release it as the horse responds correctly. If he does not respond appropriately to light pressure, stronger, uncomfortable pressure is applied and maintained until the horse reacts correctly. Pressure gives him a problem to solve – how to relieve it. Therefore the pressure has to be appropriate for each action the rider requires. It has to be exact and constructed to give the horse no choice, but one correct answer only. He thus learns correctly from the first trial. The pressure is only (and *instantly*) removed when the horse yields or reacts correctly. This timely release of pressure rewards, encourages and thus reinforces each correct reaction. It tells the horse that he has solved the problem and that his reaction is correct. Horses learn fast and remember that light pressure precedes strong, uncomfortable pressure. This teaches them to consistently choose the correct response: they learn that yielding to light pressure is by far the favoured option and they thus react immediately to exquisitely light aids. The training is shortened by years.

Rein pressure is applied by making a fist.

The hand softens as the horse yields.

Timing of pressure-release

The most important aspect of a pressure-release system is that the timing of the release corresponds perfectly with the timing of the horse's correct reaction. When the pressure is released a split second before the desired outcome, the horse learns nothing. If the release is more than three seconds late, or is after an incorrect response, the reward will be for the wrong reaction and the horse learns the incorrect response. For example, if you ask the horse to give one forward step, but you only apply stopping knee pressure after two steps, the horse will have understood that the request was for two steps. If the timing of the release is late, the horse becomes insensitive to pressure. This is how hard mouths, so-called 'lazy' horses or insensitive horses are rider-made. This system has not always been understood, learnt or executed correctly by most riders. Their communications thus often lack clarity to their horses. The timing of the pressure-release can either teach the horse to yield or, when the timing is incorrect, the horse teaches the rider to yield when he pulls. He realises that if he pulls hard enough, the rider will yield.

SIV AND MARIELLE'S horses had developed tossing reactions as their riders took up or shortened the reins. (This is a common rider problem). The dentist and vet were called in, but no health problems could be found. In both cases the reins were released when the tossing commenced; the horses were thus rewarded for head-tossing.

Horses generally have a pre-emptive head movement before the tossing. In Marielle's case the horse lifted his neck very slightly before the tossing. Siv's horse made a slight downwards pre-emptive nod. Once these pre-emptive movements were pointed out, both riders could recognise and feel them. This gave them the one second they needed to prepare for the pressure-release action. They had to 'lock' both arms and fists as the horse made his pre-emptive movement (an action explained further in Chapter 11). The horse would then 'bump' into the bit at the first toss. The pressure was released the instant he relaxed his head. Both the horses became completely relaxed in a steady, round 'on the bit' frame after three tossing attempts. (See note 6 on page 186)

Good feel and coordination (technique) are essential and timing is crucial because sometimes you have to react to the start of the yielding as you feel the horse is about to/begins to react correctly. At other times you release only when the horse has yielded fully.

Rein pressure has been described over the centuries using a variety of words, all referring to the same concept. They include 'take and give', 'hold and release', 'sponge', 'vibrate', 'feather', 'squeeze and release' and even, 'feel the reins'. Calf and knee pressure is usually described as 'squeeze and release'; seat pressure as 'push'.

Introduce the pressure at the first sign of resistance. Release the pressure completely and instantly as the horse yields or he will resist increasingly at each repetition of the pressure. He will finally be dull to the aids, not move forwards and not stop. He is then said to be 'resistant'. Trainers can help to improve rider reaction time by calling attention to the change in the horse and insisting on a reaction.

One of the most common problems is evident in the half-halt. Riders are extremely reluctant to yield completely after a slowing down half-halt. Some tension remains on the reins, which prevents the horse from learning to slow down. This release of pressure is not sufficient for the horse to feel rewarded.

SUSAN COULD NOT slow down her highly trained pony sufficiently on hacks. Finally, in a very safe environment, she relaxed completely after the half-halt: her reins became loopy. To her surprise, the pony responded by slowing down into an extremely slow, collected canter. The problem disappeared once she realised that the cause had always been her reluctance to release the reins completely after each half-halt.

Reward plays a major part in learning.[6] The release of pressure, together with another positive or concrete reward such as a tickle on the withers, a food titbit or simple verbal praise, improves clarification to the horse. It teaches in a positive manner and speeds up the learning process. A clicker or 'voice' clicker (a single word) can also be added for clearer understanding. Horses only need three repetitions to understand new work if it is rewarded appropriately.

TO SQUARE-UP THE horse's forelegs the rider needs to maintain calf pressure and regulating rein pressure until the last step is squared out. Michelle's horse habitually took one step back immediately after squaring up his forelimbs at the halt because she maintained the rein pressure too long after releasing calf pressure. The problem was solved when Michelle's timing and multi-tasking improved.

Principles of pressure-release technique

Apply the lightest leg pressure to which you would like the horse to react. If he does not react to this light pressure, follow up immediately with strong enough pressure for an immediate reaction. This may be a tap with the whip, which results in immediate reaction, or increasingly stronger spur pressure (not spur-tapping) until the horse reacts, then release instantly. Continuous spur-tapping constitutes nagging and is more than one aid – the horse thus learns to ignore the spurs. Spur use should never be *instead of* leg use because this leads to habituation to the spurs. Using stronger leg pressure without the use of spurs also leads to continuous nagging, which the horses soon learn to ignore. The tap with the whip should be strong enough to elicit the correct reaction from the horse, but not so strong that it elicits an over-reaction. Chapter 11 describes the pressure-release technique for rein aids.

The meaning of aids (pressure) to the horse

Horses have to learn to yield to two basic instructions. They have to yield to leg pressure by taking steps and they have to yield to bit pressure. All schooled movements are variations of these two reactions to pressure.

1. Calf pressure should mean 'take forward steps'.

2. Unilateral leg pressure should mean 'take lateral steps'.

3. Knee pressure, if taught by following up with rein pressure, should mean 'stop forward movement'.

4. Two-handed rein pressure should mean 'stop forward movement'.

5. Unilateral inside rein pressure should mean 'bend the neck'.

6. Unilateral leg pressure on the ribs, together with unilateral rein pressure on the same side, should mean 'bend'.

7. Unilateral sideways rein pressure should mean 'move the shoulder sideways' (either in or out, depending on the direction of the pressure).

8. Soft, vibrating rein pressure should mean 'yield into the round flexor 'on the bit' frame, or 'bend'.

Chapter 5

||||||||||||||||||||||||||||||||||||||||||||||||||||||||||||||||||||||||||||||||||||||||||||||||||||||||||||||||||||||||||||||||||||||||||||||||||||||||||||||||||||||||

LEARNING FEEL

ALTHOUGH FEEL MAY take years to perfect, it should be taught from the outset of learning to ride: the more feel awareness is taught, the more it develops. Riders will only achieve the almost invisible communication with the horse once feel has been developed to the highest degree and the rider can feel the tiniest incipient unwanted action from the horse and act to prevent it.

It has been proved that information about three-dimensional physical activities (such as riding) is substantially better understood and remembered when it is felt rather than when it is only seen or heard.[1] Using the kinaesthetic and tactile perceptions is thus essential in the learning and teaching of riding. If you can feel the sensation in your body, you can re-create the sensation and produce the correct response.

DEVELOPING FEEL

The development of feel follows the same sequence as learning all new skills. A practical example from riding is as follows.

1. At first you cannot feel the leading leg in canter. In fact, you do not even realise that there *is* a leading leg in canter. (Unconscious incompetence).

2. You understand that the horse leads with the right limbs when on right-handed circles and with the left limbs on left-handed circles, but you cannot yet feel,

without looking down, with which leg the horse is leading; you have to peek down to check. (Conscious incompetence).

3. You can feel, without looking down, with which leg the horse is leading, and can consciously position the horse to take the correct lead, but you cannot prevent an incorrect lead if the horse manoeuvres out of position. (Conscious competence).

4. When your feel is fully developed your reactions are automatic. You can feel whether the horse will take the correct lead before the first stride and prevent the incorrect lead automatically. It becomes second nature and you can multi-task. This is the stage when hand, finger and leg movements become invisible and we can pre-empt the horse's incorrect actions. It is proof that feel can be taught and developed. (Unconscious competence).

GRETHA, A VERY novice rider on an experienced horse, was learning to ride shoulder-in. The movement had been explained and demonstrated to her and she had been taught all the necessary techniques to perform it. Although she was executing the movement correctly with the correct body use, she stopped suddenly and exclaimed, 'I have no idea what I am doing, why I am doing it, or what I am supposed to feel.' Without knowing the feeling or what to feel, she did not understand the concept nor what she was doing. She was in the first phase of learning. Chunking, the development of gross and fine motor coordination, repetition and reinforcement of the correct feel of every step of the movement, solved the problem.

Feel develops according to the same principles of learning coordination. It develops from large to small (at first you can only feel large differences), slow to fast (you initially take a long time to feel the differences) and simple to complex (you cannot initially feel complex changes such as engagement). Mileage, correct practice and repetition are needed to develop good feel. Riders then learn to feel the horse's reaction to many situations and therefore learn to anticipate and correct before mistakes are made. Technique and timing become automatic through the development of feel and coordination. It becomes like driving a car. The corrections require no conscious thought.

TEACHING AND LEARNING FEEL

Verbal language, especially vague language, falls short when it comes to teaching feel. Feel is a non-representative entity: one rider cannot feel exactly what another feels. Each person has their own unique way of imparting what they personally feel and mere words are inadequate to represent and translate this feeling perfectly. It is almost like explaining colour to a blind person.

SAM SAID THAT her riding school teacher used to say, 'Feel that', when something was randomly correct, or even when something was wrong. She could, however, not feel anything at all because, without the physical representation, she had no idea of what the sensation was supposed to be.

Feel cannot be taught through the visual modality of demonstration. It can only be taught by giving the rider the experience of feel. Riding should thus be taught through a multi-sensory method.

KATHY COULD NOT maintain a continuous curve when riding a circle. She was first given verbal instructions, after which these were repeated as she was riding. They included inside rein vibrations. However, the circle did not improve. She appeared to understand the instruction correctly and she thought that she was vibrating the rein. However, there were so many other actions to think about and to do that she forgot to vibrate it. Only after the actions were demonstrated in detail (visual) and she experienced the correct feel sensations on the reins, could she integrate them and ride the circle correctly. The verbal instructions alone had little effect.

The role of the trainer

Trainers have to become feel-aware and constantly give riders awareness of the detail of the feeling of the correct movement, and also the feeling as faults start to appear. Only trainers who have good body awareness and understand feel (and can remember the lack thereof when they themselves started riding) can convey the correct feel. This allows riders to find the closest feel representation to that which the trainer attempts to impart.

Riders have to learn feel-sensitivity to changes of balance, rhythm, muscle tone, body position, contact, straightness, impulsion, collection and engagement.

Learning/teaching techniques for experiencing feel

Using the trained horse

Riders cannot know what to feel, or reproduce the correct feel, if they have not been given the opportunity to experience it. The best method of experiencing correct feel is to learn on a superbly trained horse. Unfortunately, this is seldom possible because finding superbly trained horses is a little like finding hens' teeth. Once riders have experienced the correct sensations, they will know how to 'search' for and recognise them again. When they learn on trained horses, they have a yardstick for comparison when they are trying to introduce movements such as shoulder-in, piaffe and pirouettes on untrained horses.

Setting up the horse

If a trained horse is not available, a competent trainer should ride the horse for a few minutes to set him up correctly, for example to correct his contact or a shoulder-in. The pupil then rides the horse immediately afterwards to experience the correct feel. The horse will retain this for only a few days or until the rider 'teaches' him incorrectly again. (Horses learn or relearn from every rider, good or bad, every time they are ridden.)

SHERYL'S HORSE HAD been trained abusively by two men before she had bought him. He thus became afraid of men, taking a wide berth around them while the whites of his eyes showed. I suggested that male riders should not ride him during his re-schooling to softer aids. I was away for two weeks and in her first lesson after my return, I rode the horse. The change in his contact was immediately noticeable although I did not know that a man had ridden him. When I reminded her of our deal she could not believe that I had felt the difference. I had, in fact, felt the stronger contact of the male touch even though the horse was only ridden once by the male trainer.

Learning from the horse's habits

Horses have very predictable habits and reactions as explained in Chapter 4. Use these repetitive reactions to your advantage to learn feel. When you are learning to ride the horse in a round frame, you will find that he repeatedly becomes 'soft' and accepting at the same spot of the circle or the arena. He will also lift his head at another spot repeatedly. When you know what to expect and where to expect it, you can learn to feel the correct sensation, the incorrect one and the process of change. You can prepare to feel it in advance and thus learn to prevent it. For example, you will immediately feel when the horse is soft but, after approximately a quarter of a circle, he may start to lift his head, either to look at something or to adjust his balance. Consequently, you feel the correct contact as well as the incorrect contact within one circle. Increase the length of time the horse maintains the correct contact by preventing him from lifting his nose. Use small 'take and give' finger and/or hand actions shortly before the spot where the horse usually lifts his head. Once the horse loses the round flexor frame, it will be more difficult to regain it and you will have to use stronger rein aids. The horse, however, will become soft again at the same spot on the circle as before, so you can begin again. Turning this into a challenge to try to complete an entire circle in the round, 'on the bit', flexor frame, will provide motivation for riders to concentrate and feel with intent. If this head-lifting is prevented successfully, the horse will maintain steadiness after three correct interventions.

Body and feel awareness

Good body awareness is essential to learning feel. Both trainer and rider have to be in tune with their tactile and kinaesthetic senses and become 'body and feel aware'. You have to learn to feel how the horse affects each body part. You have to 'put your brain into your hands and think with your fingers', so to speak. Only by becoming aware of your body parts and their movements, can you become aware of the effect of your actions on the horse, and his on you. You then become seemingly still – increasing awareness assists in developing 'invisible' movements. Without this awareness, riders use more and larger movements when learning new skills.

Riders also have to become aware of how horses perceive the pressure of the aids. Imagine yourself as a horse; imagine how the horse experiences the rider's leg pressure in different positions; imagine your meaningful and non-meaningful movements on the horse, the bit and the pressure or pain it causes. This gives feel awareness, but also respect for the horse's ability to understand vague riding language.

Close your eyes and try to become aware of every individual part of your body and where it is. This is the sense of proprioception. Start with your fingers and toes and then slowly move through your entire body. Your body parts are easier to feel when you move them or contract the muscles.

With your eyes closed, touch different body parts with each hand and note which hand is better at locating the exact point. For example, touch the tip of your nose or the point of your elbow. Lift both arms straight in front of your body. Try to hold them parallel. Open your eyes to check whether they are indeed parallel.

In most cases, they are not. This is because we are not ambidextrous. The better the development of your non-dominant hand, the more your arms will mirror each other. Other variations of this exercise are to place your arms sideways or above your head and check whether they are indeed parallel.

What to feel through your seat

Riders can ascertain the correctness of the horse's movements and position through pressure changes in their own bodies. It is complicated to feel where the horse's feet are or what he is doing; it is easier to feel the effect the horse has on your body. Feel this with closed eyes until you are sure of the sensations.

1. Feel the rhythm and the change in rhythm. This could be problematic if you don't have good rhythm. Use music, with the correct beat, or a metronome to maintain a rhythm in walk, trot and canter.

2. Feel the speed of the movement. This is your kinaesthetic sense.

3. Feel the engagement of the hindquarters. This is difficult at first, but eventually you will feel the hind hooves clearly pushing the ground more underneath your seat. You will feel more cadence/bounce in the hindquarters. Horses all bounce more after learning their first lateral movements. Use this to experience the feel.

4. Feel the length of stride in walk. Your hips will move more forwards and back as the horse takes longer strides.

5. Feel the forelegs move in the walk. Your hips move left and right together with the forelegs. You feel pressure on your seat bones when the hind legs are in mid stance.

6. Feel the widening of the hind legs (if they do widen). Wide hind legs push your seat up.

7. Feel the squareness of the hind legs in the halt. It is helpful to know the feeling of a square halt if you do not have mirrors. Both your seat bones feel the same pressure and both your hip bones are level when the horse's hind legs are square. The asymmetric pressure, when the hind legs are not square, is variable depending on the exact position of the horse's legs. You may either feel more pressure on one seat bone or a lowered hip and foot/stirrup on one side when the halt is not square behind. This hip position is quite visible, especially when one hind leg is well back.

8. Feel the inside bend. Your outside hip drops slightly and you should feel more pressure on your inside seat bone. Also feel the horse 'worm' out under your seat to the inside.

9. Feel the consistency of the angle in the half-pass. When it is consistent, your outside seat bone moves back and maintains its position. It moves forwards when the hindquarters trail.

10. Feel the tightening of the horse's topline. Bumping becomes more evident and shoots up your spine. Your seat becomes looser.

11. Feel the effect of the canter lead on your body. It turns your hips in the direction of the leading leg. Your weight shifts slightly to the outside, moving your inside seat bone slightly forwards. Proof of this is that the saddle only slips to the outside during canter.

12. Feel the suspension in canter and passage. Your whole body rises with the horse.

The passage.

below Use a kitchen scale to feel the correct degree of contact.

What to feel through your hands

1. The correct contact. This should ideally be between 150 and 200g (approx. 5–7oz). Neither partner should pull. However, it may be as light as the weight of the reins and often becomes stronger than 200g (7oz) during half-halts. To experience the feel of this level of contact, place a kitchen scale on a stool. Drape a strap over it and readjust the scale to 0. Pull on both sides of the strap as you read the weight of your pull.

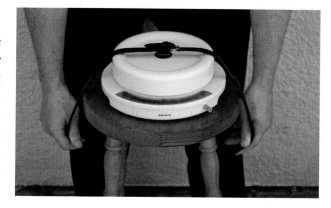

2. The feeling just before the horse lifts his head. The pressure increases on your ring fingers.

3. Unyielding contact (resistance), hanging (insensitive mouth). A heavy feeling of pulling on your arms.

4. The feeling of the horse behind the vertical avoiding bit pressure. A 'feeling' of nothing.

5. The inside bend. The inside rein has little or no feel; the outside will be straight and the feeling positive.

6. The position and control of the outside shoulder. The contact on your outside rein becomes stronger and that on the inside softer.

7. Loss of balance. The reins tighten because the horse lifts his head to balance.

8. The horse on his forehand. The reins feel heavy in your hands.

above left The reins feel tight when the horse is on the forehand.

above right The contact is soft when the horse is engaged.

What to feel through your legs

1. The inside bend. Feel a slight bulge against your outside leg.

2. Resistance to lateral movements. Too much pressure against your leg.

3. Resistance to forward movement. You have to push harder for a reaction.

4. The square halt of the forelegs. Your thigh and calf positions feel equal. When one leg is trailing, your knee on the same side will be further back than your other knee.

5. The canter lead. It places your inside leg slightly forwards and your outside leg slightly back. Feel the discomfort when you swap leg and hip positions during the canter by placing your inside leg and hip back and your outside leg and hip forwards.

Feeling the quality of the rein and leg aids

You have to know instinctively how, and with what quality, to give an aid. You can only do this if you are given the opportunity to feel it. You have to know the following instinctively.

Rein aids

1. How hard to squeeze the rein.

2. How long to hold the squeeze.

3. How many times to repeat the squeezes.

4. The length of the intervals between the squeezes.

5. How fast to vibrate.

Leg aids

1. How much leg to use for the forward aid, and for how long to maintain the pressure. This is not necessarily the same each time.

2. When to ask for more bend.

3. How hard to push for the lateral movements.

4. How strongly you should squeeze your knees for the slowing down half-halt, and how long to hold it. This is different for each half-halt depending on the horse's sensitivity at the time.

5. How often to do a half-halt.

Feel exercises through your seat

Most of the following exercises teach feel more effectively if they are performed with closed eyes. The pressure of the seat bones on the saddle is an important point of reference to develop feel. You feel weight changes through your seat bones, and so does the horse. You can feel the deep seat, but also the pressure of your individual seat bones on the saddle. When you understand the meaning of this pressure in different movements, it will form part of your 'feel' repertoire. It is felt best at the walk.

1. Place your hands on your hipbones, at walk, sitting trot and canter to feel their exact movement.

2. Alternate lifting your 'hips' (seat bones) off the saddle to experience the pressure of the deeper hip on the saddle. Roll your hips sideways by lifting the opposite hip.

3. At walk, lift both legs, knees fully flexed. Your seat bones will press into the saddle and you will be able to feel exactly how the horse places each hind leg.

4. At walk, relax your waist to allow movement and feel how your seat moves with the saddle and your shoulders become still. Tighten your waist and feel your shoulders moving forwards and back from your hips. Collapse your waist and feel the movement of your upper body increase.

5. At sitting trot, feel how the horse moves your pelvis up, down, forwards, backwards, and from side to side. Do this on the lunge with closed eyes.

6. Roll your seat bones backwards and forwards and feel how your pubic bone lifts away from the saddle and lowers towards the saddle. This is how the shifting of weight influences the horse.

7. Contract your seat muscles very tightly by pinching your buttock cheeks together. Feel how this pushes your seat out of the saddle. Relax your seat muscles completely and feel this relaxation deepening your seat more than before the contraction.

8. Contract your thigh adductors tightly against the saddle. Relax them again. This relaxation deepens your seat.

9. At walk, compare the difference in your waist movement when you stretch your spine up, to when you relax your upper back. Your waist movement increases when your upper back is relaxed/slouching. This could cause back strain. Your core muscles maintain the upward stretch position. Their contraction decreases your waist movement without causing tension. Used in sitting trot, this will help you to maintain good posture, without excessive waist movement and bouncing. Your seat will continue to maintain contact with the saddle.

Correlating feel with the visual clues

Riders should initially correlate their feel with visual clues to assist their assessment and development of correct feel. Mirrors are ideal for this but, if you don't have them, you can use the following methods.

1. **The round flexor, 'on the bit' frame.** Correlate the correct feeling of the soft contact of this frame with your eyes. You may have to look at the horse's head until the feeling is established. If you lift your gaze prematurely you may lose the contact and the frame. This sets in motion a vicious circle in which the contact becomes inconsistent. A consistent contact is of more importance than the position of your own head and eyes. Progress to feeling without looking.

2. **The correct inside bend.** Correlate the soft feel on the inside rein with your vision. You will see the tendons and inside neck muscles of the horse contracting. If the neck is smooth, the bend and feel are incorrect.

The inside neck muscles and tendons are defined in a correct bend, and the inside rein is soft.

3. **The outside diagonal.** One of the first sensations a rider has to learn to feel is riding on the outside diagonal in trot. Change diagonals to compare the difference in feel. Look at the horse's outside shoulder to correlate the feel of the correct diagonal in trot: watch it until you can correlate the feel with the visual clues. Close your eyes to internalise the feeling. Immediate feedback every time a rider is on the incorrect diagonal leads to faster automatic feel recognition. Riders should, themselves, identify which diagonal they are on; it should not be pointed out.

4. **Leg-yielding.** Leg-yield with the horse's head facing the wall. Look back at the sharp angle between the wall and the horse. During leg-yield with the hindquarters against the wall you should look back over your outside shoulder to see the sharp angle between the horse and the wall. When doing the movement

across the arena, look over your outside shoulder – it gives you a better view of the angle. Your body will correct the angle automatically and correlate it with your vision.

5. **Travers.** Assess the movement by comparing the angles of the hindquarters with the wall.

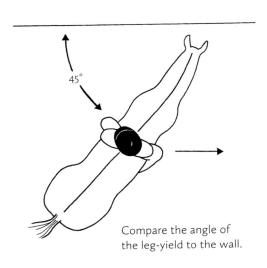

Compare the angle of the leg-yield to the wall.

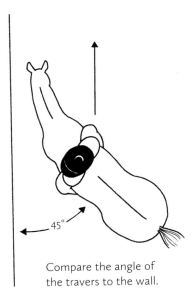

Compare the angle of the travers to the wall.

6. **Half-pass.** Assess whether the horse's hindquarters are leading or trailing in half-pass by looking over your *outside* shoulder. Your body will correct the angle automatically and your feel will be consolidated. The precise angle and position of the horse's hindquarters cannot be assessed by looking over your *inside* shoulder.

7. **The canter lead.** Correlate the feeling in your legs, pelvis and shoulders with the visual picture by looking at the horse's shoulders. Also correlate the feel and sensations of the bend and the angle of the horse's shoulders with your eyes. Store the feeling and compare it with subsequent canters.

8. **Shoulder-in.** When the horse starts to move off the track, look over your *outside shoulder* to assess the angle of the hindquarters with the track, and their distance from it. Correlate this with your feel. You will not be able to assess the distance and angle by looking over your *inside shoulder.*

9. **Halt.** Correlate the feel of the forelegs in the square halt by looking at the horse's shoulders. The shoulders will be parallel when the horse's forefeet are squared up.

10. **Counting steps.** By counting steps, you learn to feel them. The easiest way is to start by counting steps in each trot stride, 1,2;1,2. Then in the walk strides, 1,2,3,4; 1,2,3,4. Initially you will only feel the forelegs. By counting the foreleg steps you will become aware of the hind leg steps. These are easier to feel if you bend your knees and lift your legs up. Finally count the canter steps and take note of the feel of the suspension phase, 1,2,3 pause;1,2,3 pause. Bareback riding allows riders to feel the footfalls in the walk and into the halt with greater ease.

Feeling the movement in your body

New movements should be experienced off the horse. This gives riders a representative feeling of the horse's movement. For example:

1. 'Gallop' on your own feet, with each of your legs leading.

2. Circle at the gallop with the correct leading leg. Then circle in the opposite direction in 'counter-gallop' and feel how the discordant bend in your body changes your balance. Repeat with the other leg and feel the difference between your dominant and non-dominant legs.

3. Do a flying change and note how you have to hop in one spot to change. Note the automatic change of bend in your waist to change leads.

4. Walk up the track in a shoulder-in position.

5. Do half-pass, on all fours, and feel the effect on your balance at each step.

6. Jog and halt to feel how to square-up the halt.

7. Walk backwards in a flexor frame and in an extensor frame and feel the difference.

Riding with closed eyes

The next step in learning feel, is to cut out the visual clues. Riding with closed eyes is one of the most effective methods of learning feel. The development of our thinking brain has negated our dependence on our tactile and kinaesthetic senses; we have become reliant on our eyes for most things in life. Vision blocks the use of our other senses. It is notable that blind people have extremely well-developed tactile and kinaesthetic senses. They use the tactile sense for reading (Braille) and their kinaesthetic sense to find their way around the house and to their office.

Riders feel less and do not interpret what they feel when they *rely* on visual clues. By closing our eyes, we learn to rely on feel to give us the required information: We become more feel aware.

I HAVE TAUGHT A few riders with disabilities, including blindness and deafness. All had superior feel because their disabilities made them more reliant on feel.

Do the following exercises with closed eyes on a lead or lunge rein in an enclosed arena: Do them first at walk and, once you can feel the sensations, progress to the trot.

1. Feel as the rhythm changes; verbalise this and learn to react with a half-halt or leg aid as you feel this change.

2. Feel various sensations. Feel which forelimb is taking the step in the walk, the trot, the square halt and the canter lead. Verbalise these sensations.

3. Feel the horse's position for a correct canter depart. Verbalise this feeling.

4. Feel the hind legs, especially the outside hind leg into the halt.

5. Feel and correct crookedness in the halt on the centre line.

6. Feel the sensation when your horse's hindquarters are leading or trailing in leg-yield and half-pass. Feel the angle of the shoulder-in.

7. Feel the different sensations the horse's head movements have on your fingers. Your trainer should help you to experience this by lifting or dropping the horse's head and by bending it to each side.

8. Ask the horse to yield to bit pressure. This should place his head and neck in the round flexor position. Verbalise when the horse is in this submissive frame and the moment the contact hardens or becomes too soft.

9. Repeat the above exercise and feel this lightness on the reins. Your trainer should now lift the horse's nose a centimetre and ask if you can feel this. Once you can feel the horse's head move a centimetre away from your hands, open your eyes. Your teacher should show you the almost imperceptible change in the horse's head position. Your trainer should then slowly lift the horse's head to demonstrate how this small movement becomes the large head and neck lift. The horse starts hollowing from this tiny initial movement until he is in the head up, hollow extensor frame. In this position, you need corrections with large or strong hand and arm movements. Therefore, you have to learn to react, by simply closing your fingers, the instant you feel this slight rein pressure of the centimetre lift on your ring fingers. This prevents the horse from lifting his head further. Do not wait for the pressure on your ring fingers to become stronger.

The feel of the 'on the bit' position.

Feel the 1cm lift which leads to ...

... a large lift.

10. Feel the softness of the inside rein in the correct inside bend. Feel the change of pressure on the ring finger of your inside hand when the bend changes. Feel how the outside rein becomes softer as the bend changes. Verbalise this and learn to react immediately to correct the bend with your inside leg pushing the ribcage and soft squeezes on the inside rein.

Feel the rein pressure softening when the bend changes.

11. Feel the positive contact on the outside rein (150–200g/5–7oz). Verbalise the feel and learn to react immediately should it change. React with the pushing inside leg and 'take and give' on the inside hand. Feel the outside rein moving the horse's shoulders.

12. Feel the canter lead. Once you can recognise the correct lead, ask the horse to canter and close your eyes for a few strides to feel it. Try to ascertain which leg is leading. Feel the difference between the correct and incorrect lead. If the horse is on the incorrect lead, continue on a circle and feel the discomfort. Use this to build your feel memory.

13. Practise the 'aids', all the techniques of communication as described in later chapters, with your eyes closed.

14. Ride movements such as shoulder-in or walk pirouette with closed eyes. It will illuminate every aid you give and every response the horse gives in return.

TINA FELT THAT SHE was co-contracting her shoulder girdle every time she started to correct her horse, but could not prevent it. Riding with her eyes closed highlighted the sensation. She could thus verbalise it and then prevent the co-contraction before starting the movement.

The success of this method depends on the trainer's ability to observe and point out the change in the horse and rider through verbal feedback. Only then will the rider know which feeling is correct. Your trainer should ask questions regarding the effect of the movement on your body. For example, answer questions such as which hip and leg are in a more forward position.

'Hands on' to experience feel

Riders need 'hands on' (kinaesthetic and tactile) experience to understand riding terminology and feel. Ask your trainer to use 'hands on' to give you feel experience though the following exercises.

Mounted exercises

1. Feel which muscles to contract when your trainer touches them. For example, the trainer could 'draw' connections, with two fingers between the tips of your shoulder blades. You will immediately feel which muscles to contract to straighten your upper body.

The trainer can trace the rhomboid muscles (see page 141) to help the pupil identify which muscles to contract.

2. Your trainer should walk next to you, while cupping your hands, to give you the correct feel and timing of your finger or hand movements on the reins as the horse moves.

3. Your trainer can place a hand between the horse's ribcage and your leg. Give each leg aid against the hand so your trainer can correct your pressure and give you the correct feel.

above left The trainer holding the pupil's hands to help the pupil experience the required feeling.

above right The trainer placing a hand between the horse's ribcage and the pupil's leg to check the quality of the leg aid.

4. Your trainer should use their hands against your calf to demonstrate:
   - The principle of feeling changes of pressure.
   - Different pressure strengths of the leg aids.
   - The quality of passive leg contact against the horse.
   - The technique and timing of the leg aids.

5. Your trainer should push against your calf to move the horse's weight to the other side. Hold the reins at equal length, but do not move them. You will immediately feel the contact on the outside rein, the soft inside rein and the inside bend. You will feel the horse's weight shift. This is the feeling you experience as you ask for the canter.

6. Your trainer should push against the horse's shoulder to move his weight onto his opposite leg. Feel the weight change and try to reproduce this positioning of

the horse with your inside leg in a forward position, or give a whip tap on the horse's shoulder to encourage him to move his shoulder out. See also Chapter 9.

7. Your trainer should give you the feeling of the positioning into the correct canter depart by:
   • Pushing the horse's ribcage or shoulder to the outside.
   • Positioning the horse at the halt so that his inside shoulder is leading. You should be able to see this, then learn to feel it. Feel and verbalise how this position affects your body.
   • Pointing out the changes in the horse as you take the canter depart. For example, his quarters may swing out to change his weight distribution, his bend or lead.

The trainer pushing the horse's shoulder to give the pupil the feeling of the horse's weight change as well as the accompanying inside bend.

Dismounted exercises

Dismounted exercises can help you to experience the horse's movements. When teaching a new movement, trainers should manoeuvre the pupil into the correct position. For example, in teaching the correct positioning of the horse for a canter depart, the trainer should place their hands on each side of the pupil's waist and bend it slightly to one side, then turn the pupil's hips in the correct direction so that the inside leg leads. The pupil's weight should be pushed onto the 'outside' leg.

For half-pass, the pupil's waist should be bent, the hips turned and the outside leg pushed to cross over the inside leg.

Sally Swift's game of mirror hands[2] teaches you the feel of coordinating your hands with and anticipating the horse's fast reactions, as though through the reins. Start the exercise with your eyes closed to ensure that you rely completely on your feel. (Once you can follow the movement smoothly, repeat it with open eyes – it seems to be more difficult when your eyes are open.) Place the palms of both your hands against your trainer's palms. Your trainer should move their hands individually or together in any direction, while you follow them and maintain perfect soft contact. There should be no pressure, just light, consistent touch, as in praying. You may not anticipate by pushing your hands or snapping them away too fast, neither should you lag behind. Practise this until you can follow your trainer's movements smoothly without losing contact, in whichever direction and speed their hands move. If you have any residual tightness in your elbows, you will not be able to follow your trainer's hands. When you can follow perfectly at the halt, repeat the exercise while walking with your trainer. Change leaders for more understanding.

right Manoeuvring the pupil in half-pass. Here, the pupil is losing balance because her shoulders have moved laterally beyond her base of support. The horse can lose balance in the same manner in this movement.

far right Mirror hands.

Use of the reins to give riders the correct feel

Riders should learn to feel the effect of their fingers on the reins and the classical pressure-release system of rein communication early in training. This helps to prevent the detrimental actions of hanging, pulling, fiddling and sawing on the horse's mouth, which stunt the rider's ability to feel the communication from the horse. Riders misunderstand rein use mainly because of vague teaching language.

Holding the reins between trainer and rider

Trainers should give riders the closest possible representation of feel by teaching them to react to the smallest nuances of movements on the rein. These prevent the horse from lifting his nose, through lack of submission, loss of attention, or loss of balance.

This method of learning feel is very effective. It should be repeated whenever the rider's contact is faulty. The trainer should hold the reins close to the horse's mouth. Enough space should be allowed so as not to interfere with the bit. The rider holds the other ends of the reins about 15cm (6in) from the buckle. The rider should first feel with closed eyes and then with open eyes while the trainer tweaks the reins, as lightly as possible. The reins should be squeezed with diminishing qualities of pressure until the rider can feel a nuance of movement without looking.

The trainer demonstrating the correct rein pressure to the mounted rider. This exercise can also be done dismounted.

The trainer giving the rein actions

The trainer should move the reins as though they were the horse's head and demonstrate:

The correct elastic contact. The trainer should move the reins while the rider's hands follow, smoothly and without anticipation. The trainer must ensure that the rider can maintain a consistent contact with elastic arm movements. It is useful to repeat the mirror hands exercise above, with the reins held between trainer and rider, initially with the rider's eyes closed then, once the feeling of consistent yielding elastic contact is established, with the eyes open.

A stronger contact, as the horse would do when leaning on the bit, becoming hollow, or losing the inside bend. The rider has to learn to react immediately as the trainer changes the contact.

The strength, timing and feel of each rein aid. The rider's hands will feel what the horse feels in his mouth and should then respond to these sensations. Starting with the ideal end product of the lightest invisible squeezing, the following are replicated:

- The visible take and give.

- Feathering/vibrating the reins.

- Holding the contact by closing a fist, and releasing as the horse would yield.

- Emulating rider resistance.

The rider giving the rein actions

- Trainer and rider should then swop roles, the rider now demonstrating the actions and the trainer correcting them. The trainer:

- Demonstrates the feel of a relaxed yet responsive mouth by relaxing their arms. The rider gives the 'aids' which the trainer feels and follows as a horse with perfect contact should.

- Corrects these 'aids' if the feel is incorrect. Tension, timing and the quality of pressure from the rider's hands, arms or shoulders should be corrected.

- Resists the rider's 'aids' as a horse would, then demonstrates how to coax a 'resisting horse' to yield.

- Demonstrates the feel and timing of instant yielding to pressure.

- Demonstrates how the rider should react instantly and effectively to the horse's sudden changes of contact. The trainer should try to 'catch out the rider' by 'losing contact' (pushing the reins towards the rider's hands), 'becoming hollow' or 'hardening the contact'.

Once riders have learnt to become aware of the sensations, they soon learn to react automatically.

Dismounted rein exercises

The above exercises can also be done dismounted. Use a pair of reins attached to a bit, between you and your trainer and take turns in giving and receiving the rein 'aids' (being the rider and being the horse). Hold the bit across your palms and stand in front, with your back to your trainer. You should have no visual clues. Ask your trainer to give 'rein aids'. Feel the sensations which the horse experiences through the bit. Feel the difference between light feathering and hard pulling. Feel the lightest pressure on the bit which the horse can feel. Your trainer should demonstrate how, and how fast, to react so that you can feel the correct technique and timing of the aids. Then change places with your trainer. Close your eyes and test your reactions to different variations of contact, such as the horse lifting his head, or bend resistances. Your reactions should be fast, with the appropriate strength and variation of 'take and give'. Try to prevent the movements from becoming large. Your trainer should correct you when your 'aids' do not feel correct. Use these reins from time to time to check whether your feel remains appropriate.

Experiencing the correct rein pressure with closed eyes.

More riding movements to experience feel

Certain exercises allow riders to experience the correct feel and to remember it. The trainer should draw the rider's attention to the specifics of the feel when the horse is moving correctly. Try the following exercises.

1. Ask your trainer to point out when you are producing the best movement. For example, the most active walk. Close your eyes for a few seconds to form a memory of this feeling. This will help you to reproduce the same walk on a different occasion.

2. Bring body awareness into the equation by comparing a well-executed movement with the previously poorly executed movement. Verbalise the feel of the poor-quality movement and verbalise the feel of a correctly executed movement and then verbalise the corrections.

3. Correct transitions improve balance and engagement automatically. Start with walk-halt-walk transitions. Progress to trot-walk-trot transitions and move on to trot-halt-trot transitions when your horse yields correctly into the downward and upward transitions. If he uses his forelimbs to brake and lifts his head or hops into the trot, his hindquarters will not engage. When he uses his hindquarters correctly in the transitions he will lose the upward hop and the downward pull.

4. Walk to canter transitions on a 10m circle collect the canter automatically.

5. Lateral movements in walk improve engagement in the trot. Leg-yield, shoulder-in and quarter to full pirouettes at the walk all have this engaging effect in the trot. They also encourage the round flexor frame. Ask for trot instantly after practising these exercises. You will immediately feel the bounce of the horse's hind legs.

6. Quarter to full walk pirouettes automatically engage the horse's hindquarters to produce a more collected canter.

Chapter 6

THE AIDS – COMMUNICATING WITH THE HORSE

EFFECTIVE RIDING IS dependent on effective and detailed communication with the horse so that he can understand our every move. For this reason and because it is our duty towards these generous animals, it is essential for us to learn how they understand the rider, how they communicate *their* wishes to the rider and how they learn.

Although horses can learn to respond to a very basic human vocabulary, they are not able to understand nuances or verbal explanations. For example, they can learn to understand the word 'trot', but can they understand the phrase, 'collect the trot'? If we are to communicate effectively, this must be done through the body language of feel. How good are you at understanding body language?

UNDERLYING PRINCIPLES

The aids should request and explain to the horse exactly what we require of him, and convince him of the need to respond. Communication should thus involve meaningful persuasions and manoeuvring of the horse's automatic reactions, reinforced with pressure-release actions. This ensures that the horse understands the instructions correctly at the first time of asking – this is 'aiding' the horse. Once the horse thoroughly understands the concepts, the aids eventually become mere invisible signals. These signals constitute horse words – a proper body language.

SHORTLY BEFORE writing this I was hypnotised and taken back to 6 months of age. I was a little sceptical about how I was going to remember anything, since a baby of that age has very little in the way of language skills. The memory however, returned as emotions, visual pictures and physical sensations. The latter were the first memories to appear. My chest hurt, my throat tightened and then I saw myself lying in a cot, gurgling, giggling, kicking with my legs and making hand gestures. I was trying with all the power of a 6-month-old baby's limited communication tools, to coerce someone into picking me up. After the session, it struck me that horses have even fewer communication tools to communicate their wishes to humans. They have their emotions, their will and some physical tools which they use in their attempts to get the message across that something is wrong. Sadly, these are often ignored and misunderstood.

Some time later I was training a 3- year-old pony in her second schooling session when she did not want to move forwards to trot. I was expecting her to follow on from the first session in which she had learnt extremely quickly. However, when I put my legs on she put her ears back, tried to turn then stopped and shook her head vehemently. At first I assumed that she had a 'stubborn' streak. However, stubbornness in a horse is not in my belief system. When she finally took three trot strides I immediately felt her waddling. Further investigation revealed a strained muscle. The little darling was trying her utmost to pass on this message and I was a little slow in the uptake.

It is perhaps ironic that we expect horses to understand our non-verbal communication when we are not necessarily that proficient at communicating non-verbally with other people. What would you do if you had a mouth full of food and needed something from the cutlery drawer, but someone was standing in front of it? You might try to push them sideways away from the drawer. But not everyone would move out of the way promptly. Some would plant themselves firmly because they did not understand, or are defensive. So it is with horses. Some horses react quickly while others resist because they do not understand or are trying to communicate a problem. The more 'words' we have in our body vocabulary, the better the horse will understand us.

Although we riders need to explain our wishes clearly to our horses, we often leave them in the dark. We tend to try to communicate in mysterious and invisible ways for the sake of aesthetics and forget that the main aim is to be successful in communicating with the horse, our partner. Is there any point in anything we do in training, if the horse does not understand us?

This is why explanations have to be careful and precise and each small chunk of understanding should be rewarded. Imagine the horse's frustration when the rider uses the wrong 'words' and then punishes him for not responding correctly. We are often told that we should never use short cuts in training. If the horse understands the trainer, he learns remarkably quickly. The training process becomes dramatically shortened without these bogus 'short cuts'.

I WITNESSED A RIDER clinic in which the horse would not move forwards. The clinician tried a few methods unsuccessfully, then explained what she called 'a controversial method'. She asked the rider to halt the horse in front of her. She then gave the horse a whack under his belly with the dressage whip. The horse got the fright of his life and took a huge sideways jump. From that point on, he would not go near the trainer. He never knew why he had been hit, but only realised that he should stay clear of that human being. Ironically, this trainer could not understand why the horse would not come near her again.

In reality, the horse is the willing, or unwilling, partner who has no choice in the matter. The rider therefore carries a huge responsibility for finding appropriate communication skills to 'convince' the horse to perform correctly. If the horse performs incorrectly, the rider has failed to put the message across – the horse has not failed or been naughty. We cannot expect the horse to take the responsibility. When riders claim that their horse 'is stubborn', that 'he knows', that 'he is hanging or pulling', etc., they are expecting human responsibility from him. Even when horses are temperamentally difficult, we are still responsible for correcting this – if we can't, we are simply not good enough.

Riders probably all differ slightly in their body use when asking the horse to do a specific movement. This is not important though. What is important is that the horse understands these explanations clearly. If we adhere rigidly to specific aids which the horse may not understand, or which are not effective, what is the point of giving them at all?

COMMUNICATION, COORDINATION AND BALANCE

Riders have to be a hundred per cent clear about what they are asking of the horse. They have to be able to visualise precisely what they want from the horse and from themselves. Their bodies have to perform exactly as their minds require. Excellent balance and body awareness with well-developed fine and gross motor coordination are equally important for correct body use. These attributes allow riders to use delicate skills for precise and effective communication. Without them, clear, unambiguous communication with the horse is difficult. Our body language has to be consistently correct to avoid giving confusing mixed messages.

Timing, too, has to be perfect. If the horse does not react correctly, look for the communication error in your technique and timing of the aids. Make clear, distinguishable adjustments to your body use. For example, if you want the horse's shoulder to move away from your leg, your leg must move forwards into a position closer to the horse's shoulder, or he will misunderstand the request. If you apply pressure in the same place every time, the horse will react with the same response every time.

Correct communication

When the aids for a specific movement are ineffective, it is usually because the horse did not understand clearly enough. He may simply be resisting you, but that means that you were not convincing enough for him to accede to your intent. Never persist in actions which do not produce the desired results immediately. If it is not effective, your technique is incorrect. Try another method. You have four options when the horse does not understand the question.

1. Repeat the question. Perhaps the horse was not focusing on you fully. If he has been trotting for a long time, he may not expect a request to canter. If one repetition does not help, more will be a wasted effort.

2. 'Speak louder'. This is a light aid followed by a strong aid if the light aid is ignored.

3. Try another 'word'. This is the most successful method. If you are squeezing the rein and the horse does not yield or respond, it is pointless to continue with the same ineffective action or 'word'. Change your method of asking. Try different methods of pressure-release on the reins until you become effective and the horse understands.

4. If none of the above is effective, your techniques are incorrect and you should seek expert assistance.

Simultaneous opposing messages

Riders have been giving horses simultaneous opposing messages for centuries despite horses not understanding opposing messages. By around 370 BC Xenophon had already explained that riders should not give their horses two opposing messages. He said, 'You must refrain from pulling at his mouth with the bit and from spurring and whipping him.' He says that it 'scares them into disorder and danger' [confusion and anxiety].[1]

In 1855, a serious accident left François Baucher, who had previously been a strong and demanding rider, physically weakened. He thus developed his *deuxième manière* (second method) of using hands and legs separately. He referred in this to '*mains sans jambes, jambes sans mains*' – hands without legs; legs without hands. This means that the stopping hand aids and the going leg aids should not be used simultaneously. The horse thus receives unambiguous messages and the aids become clear and light.

Research has shown that unclear and opposing instructions (aids) give horses confusing messages. Confusion in horses leads to tension and anxiety. The 'hotter' breeds such as the Thoroughbred, Arabian and Trakehners, and young horses generally, become anxious. They receive two opposing messages when the rider's legs give forward aids while their hands give stopping instructions and when one leg gives a sideways pushing aid and the other inadvertently also pushes, even a little. No horse learns through confusion. Horses become calm when the confusion of two opposing messages is removed.

However, most riders unwittingly give their horses two simultaneous opposing messages, one to go, and another to stop. This is mainly a result of tension or inadequately developed coordination in their arms or other body parts. Tension anywhere in the rider's upper body causes bit pressure in the horse's mouth. Horses interpret bit pressure as slowing down instructions. A rider's arms tightening when only fine finger-feathering is required is an example of this slowing down bit pressure. During my many years of teaching, I have found that 99 per cent of riders have arm tightness. These riders pull back on the reins as they ask the horse to move on from the halt.

A COMMON COMMAND by riding teachers is, 'Take up the contact'. They use this phrase instead of saying, 'Shorten your reins'. Riders thus misinterpret the concept of contact and assume that it should be firm. De la Guérinière said that the horse should be directed by 'reins attracted by the concept of gravity'. Of this method Nuno Oliveira said. 'I believe this conception of lightness to be the stamp of superior equitation. It is a far cry from the methods which, under the pretext of making the horse taut like a bowstring, actually provoke and stimulate a constant traction on the reins.'[2]

The widely used method of 'riding forwards into contact' gives horses two simultaneous, but opposing, messages. There seems to be a tendency to misinterpret this phrase as pushing the horse forwards into a firm rein contact, whereas the correct interpretation is that the horse is pushed forwards to yield into a soft contact that, itself, yields. However, Racinet said, 'There cannot be such a thing as a hand that resists passively. Any form of resistance is active, and it is therefore a fact, it is the truth that the rider who "pushes onto the bit" both pushes and pulls.'[3] I believe the point he is making here is that, while the rider may be resisting passively, the horse experiences it as active bit pressure. In most hands, attempts at this method lead to defensive behaviour or anxiety in the horse from the confusion of the opposing messages. The round frame with lightness does not involve two opposing messages because there is no active bit pressure. Therefore you can ride the horse forwards, while he maintains self-carriage.

The commonly used phrase, 'forwards into halt' is another example of giving two opposing messages. This not only causes bit pressure, but when the riders' legs and hands are used together, the energy becomes locked in. The horse stops moving forwards and becomes hard in the mouth. Two opposing aids should therefore not be used to teach horses.

When hands and legs may be used simultaneously

Once horses understand the underlying concepts, the rider's hands and legs may be combined and used *almost simultaneously* to square-up the halt and for energy-producing and engaging half-halts to collect the horse, and in passage. In these uses, split seconds separate the energy-containing hand and thigh action from the forward leg action. In the half-halt the rider's hands 'catch' the energy produced by the legs. All pressure is then released. The forward activity from the hind legs is thus not blocked, but converted into 'vertical' energy. In the square halt, the hands and knees block the forward movement: a split second separates this from the calf pressure which squares up the forelimbs.

Certain circumstances and movements also require that the hands and legs are used fully simultaneously, but again this should only be done once horses understand, and are confident in, the concepts of yielding to bit pressure and moving forwards to leg pressure separately. Simultaneous instructions should only be given momentarily. For example, during moments when the horse lifts his head because of some loss of attention, both legs push him into a stronger holding contact until he yields ('bunching up'). As he yields, the pressure is instantly released. Pushing the horse forwards 'into the hands' produces stronger bit pressure. On a trained horse, this leads to faster yielding.

Simultaneous hand and leg use is an advanced ability in riders. It requires exquisite timing, technique and initial leg strength. It is thus not suitable for riders lacking leg strength. I believe that this technique, used so often in riding lessons, is one of the causes of horses developing insensitivity to the leg aids and insensitive mouths.

Simultaneous *unilateral* hand and leg pressure does not produce opposing messages. When asking for bend, the leg always pushes the ribcage over first followed, in split-second timing, with vibration on the inside rein.

The symphony of the aids

The rider's whole body (with all the limbs) represents the tools of communication to control the whole horse. The hands, legs and seat are seldom used in isolation. Since we want to affect the whole horse in all his movements we have to use our bodies in a 'symphony of aids' (instructions). Therefore exquisite body coordination is paramount. As with the instruments in an orchestra, each variation of finger, hand, arm, leg and weight movement has to be practised individually, then put together in a cohesive unit. This can also be compared to playing an organ with the feet pressing the foot pedal notes while the hands not only play the notes but also pull and push the stops.

Pre-aids, not telepathy

It is often claimed that horses have a sixth sense and can 'read our thoughts'. This is not entirely correct. They read the world around them with all their senses; they learn to feel the aids, but also the preamble to every aid – that is to say, they feel and read and learn the whole sequence of our preparatory body movements leading to our requests (aids). These are the essentially meaningless movements we make when we are thinking about performing the next exercise. These become the horse's cues, which is why some horses learn to pre-empt the rider and anticipate the movement.

Every rider unconsciously repeats the same preparation before each change of movement. They are often not aware of these preparatory actions, but the horse learns all these signs, usually without the rider's realisation. For example, a horse will learn that a certain type of half-halt will announce the canter aid, and yet another is a preparation for going into halt. When the rider takes a walk break after a long trot session, the horse anticipates that canter work will follow. When the rider takes a long break to talk to the trainer, the horse believes that the lesson is over and resents starting again.

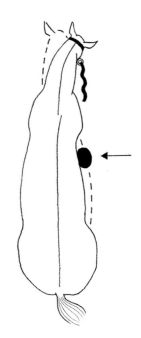

Bend is produced by inside leg pressure on the ribcage and a vibrating inside rein.

I NOTICED INTERESTING behaviour while training a young pony to canter. Before each canter I pushed my glasses firmly onto my nose to prevent them from slipping. Each time I lifted my arm to push my glasses up, Jo-jo started preparing for the canter either by speeding up, lifting her neck or by taking shorter steps. She had learnt my preamble to the canter.

Horses feel intent, tension and relaxation *through the physical effect our thoughts produce in our own bodies.* They feel every movement we make, store it in their minds as 'meaningful' or 'meaningless' and then react appropriately. Some examples of these unintentional pre-aids which are the signals or clues for the horse include:

1. The rider's breathing changes before the canter.

2. The rider shortens the reins before trot and canter.

3. The rider's muscle tone changes before giving the aids. These include finger, elbows, head/neck and weight changes.

4. The rider's head, seat, back, hips or upper body change before asking the horse to change direction.

A *little* anticipation is good because it prepares the horse for the often sudden signals (with no conscious warning preparation) given by the novice rider. The horse needs his own 'early warning' signals to protect himself against losing balance because of the generally vague or abrupt uses of the rider's 'language'. When horses are not prepared sufficiently for the movements requested they:

- Lift their heads during transitions, circles or turns.

- Run into canter.

- 'Fall' into downward transitions.

- Lean on their shoulders into the rein-back.

- Lose bend and 'fall' into turns, circles and corners.

MY FAMILY'S GREAT DANE, Suzy, goes walkabout on garbage days. She comes back stinking to high heaven. My response is to smell her with two sniffs and declare, 'Phew you stink', followed by 'Let's go bath'. This is followed by a cold shower under the garden hose. She has learnt both phrases separately and either results in her slinking out of sight. One winter I had a cold. Every time I sniffed, Suzy would slink out the room. I was puzzled at first, but finally realised that she understood the entire preamble to the cold shower including the sniff. She thus associated my sniffing from the runny nose with my sniffing to smell her.

The same principle applies to our communication with the horse. It is not only the aid which the horse understands, but everything that comes before the aid.

The Mind-Body Link

Focus, attention and the aids

Riders need focus and attention to be able to synchronise the timing of the aids and thus prevent chaos. Emotional turmoil such as PMS and tiredness may cause frustration, anger, negativity and loss of concentration. This influences the rider's timing and leads to inadequate communication and thus poor performance from the horse. It is best not to school horses under these circumstances.

The role of intent in communication

Intent is one of the most important aspects of rider-horse communication. Riders cannot expect horses to react correctly to physical signals alone until they are fully trained. The horse has to be positioned correctly to elicit a correct response but, most importantly, riders have to have intent to make it happen. Intent is determination, belief, will and concentration.

You have to think of the *result* you want to achieve rather than *what you have to do to achieve it*. You have to focus on *what you want the horse to do*, rather than on *what you must do* or how you have to give the aid. For example, if you want the horse to drop his head and neck, think of what you want him to do and try to explain it to him in a way that he will understand. Continuous repetition of a meaningless aid will have no effect. If you simply squeeze the reins randomly it becomes meaningless fiddling and nonsensical to the horse. In a similar way, if you want the horse to engage his hindquarters, lower his neck or stop hanging on the reins, you have to imagine how these messages can be put across to *convince* him to do what you require. The rein squeezes and leg aids must be meaningful so that the horse can react appropriately. *Convince* is emphasised because using this word signifies intent. For example, '*Convince* the horse to take the correct canter lead' gives intent to the rider's request and is usually very effective.

When I am certain that a rider possesses all the correct techniques and has adequate timing, yet is unable to convince their horse to do a movement, I coerce them to use intent. I inform the rider to continue riding the movement and that I shall wait until it is correct, however long it may take. This instruction never fails. It usually takes only one further attempt to achieve success because the rider does not want to keep repeating the same movement for the rest of the lesson. This is intent. It *does not* mean simply to use stronger aids.

There is a further point related to intent which might, at first sight, seem to contradict the idea mentioned earlier that horses cannot understand complex verbal commands. This is that, if you are technically able to ride a movement, and you vocalise, what you want the horse to do, he will do it. This is not, however, the horse hearing you and obeying; it is the result of your brain hearing the vocalisation of your intent and your body giving the necessary signals because your mind tells it what to do. It is a most effective method of communicating (albeit indirectly) with the horse. It speeds up rider reaction time because you have to immediately react together with your verbalisations. Your instructions become very clear when you follow your own verbalisations. It adds intent, motivation determination and correct timing to the exercise. It is important, though, that the verbalisation is out loud and not in your head. You have to hear your own instructions for auditory perception to be included in the process.

I USE THIS TECHNIQUE with great success, but often my pupils do not want to verbalise and do not believe that it could help. Nineteen-year-old Mathew could not keep the horse in a steady round flexor 'on the bit' frame. I instructed him to keep audibly telling the horse to look down or to tell him not to lift his head. He did not believe that it could work, was embarrassed to talk to his horse and thought it uncool. He also assumed that I thought the horse would listen to his voice command. It took some time for me to persuade him to do it. However, once he verbalised these phrases, the horse immediately stopped lifting his head and the contact became steady. Mathew could hardly believe the result.

Invisible communication

The ability to use invisible aids depends on three factors.

1. **Rider coordination and balance** – an independent seat – is essential for the development of invisible aids. Initially the rider's aids are very visible (large, slow and simple) until coordination, technique, timing and strength have developed. The aids then become synchronised and nuanced.

2. **Feel** has to be developed to a high degree to enable riders to respond instantly with invisible aids.

3. **The horse's level of schooling.** Riders are able to be less proactive and to communicate with smaller movements when the horse is well trained, submissive and on the aids. The aids are implied and the horse already knows what to do.

Other factors affecting communication

The 'outside' aids

These 'outside' aids are the environment in which we school horses. They include the corner of the arena, the position of the stables related to the arena, the entrance to the arena, the circle and other horses. Furthermore, the type of arena surround can also assist. Some horses concentrate better with other horses in the arena (although others may have less focus). However, it is easier to train a young horse in an indoor arena where there are no distractions and a solid wall. The wall is useful when teaching lateral movements because the horse cannot then move forwards to avoid taking a lateral step. Riding 1m away from the wall or fence teaches riders to control the horse's shoulders. Corners slow the horse down. They help riders to learn to bend the horse and to half-halt. Corners and the position of the stables can encourage horses to take the correct canter lead, after which they can associate the aid with the correct lead. If you teach a new movement in the same spot of the arena, the horse anticipates it and learns faster.

Training fads

Beware of fashionable fads in training. Gadgets, repetitive rider actions or training methods which force horses into position, move away from real communication. Fads have come and gone over the centuries. The extremely cruel and painful gadgets of the seventeenth and eighteenth centuries have thankfully disappeared. However, some modern fads are equally dangerous.

- **The 'deep and round' method** used extensively today in the form known as hyperflexion, can cause permanent physical damage to horses. It forces the horse to become oppressively submissive. Muscles stretch in only 8 seconds, but these stretches are held for minutes on end.

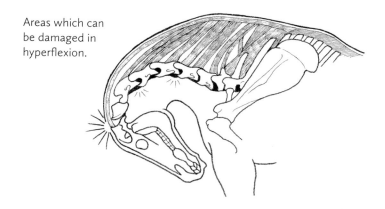

Areas which can be damaged in hyperflexion.

- **The terminology of 'inside leg to outside rein'** is confusing and often misunderstood because the phrase is biomechanically meaningless. It has led to the phrase, 'Take more outside rein' (instead of 'use more inside leg') and the practice of too strong an outside rein contact. The latter turns the horse's head and neck to the outside; he loses the inside bend and his nose twists out. Although a positive outside contact controls the horse's shoulders, no amount of taking more contact on the outside rein will produce an inside bend; the horse will simply turn his head and neck to the outside or twist his nose out. The rider then attempts to bend the horse to the inside. The result is too strong a contact on both reins and the horse becomes hard in the mouth. Bend is produced by the inside leg and inside rein. You can read more on the subject in Chapter 10 and in my book *Equine Biomechanics for Riders – The Key to Balanced Riding*.

Strong outside contact pointing the nose out.

- **The fad of squeezing with alternate reins at every stride** communicates nothing to the horse. It leads to head-swinging because the rider simply pulls the horse's head from side to side. When the horse does not yield to the pressure on the side of the squeezing fingers, his head-carriage will not become steady. It springs back to a non-yielding centre position. The rider then pulls it to the opposite side, but it simply springs back to centre position again. The sawing continues (see also Chapter 11).

- **The concept of equal contact** seems to be misunderstood. If the contact in both hands is exactly the same, the horse cannot bend. The rider will be pulling the horse around the corners, circles and turns. The bend is false and the horse does not learn to yield to inside rein pressure. The correct meaning is *equality of contact*. The contact should be the same when riding on the right rein as when riding on the left rein: it means that the horse must not have a stiff side.

These fads spread like a bush telegraph – the message becomes distorted. The original reason, which was particular to a specific horse and specific problem, disappears. The originator is copied blindly and incorrectly. Fads are better ignored and replaced with real meaningful communication with the horse.

Chapter 7

||||||||||||||||||||||||||||||||||||||||||||||||||||||||||||||||||||||||||||||||||||||||||||||||||||||||||||||||||||||||||||||||||||||||||||

THE FOUR STEPS

The four steps to riding success are four exercises which simultaneously teach riders how to coordinate their bodies and how to control their horses and they form the basis of schooling horses. All the movements, up to Grand Prix level, are variations of these four exercises.

THE FOUNDATIONS

As mentioned in Chapter 1, the two most important movements in riding are the half-halt and the shoulder-in. They form the foundation for all ridden work.

The shoulder-in position is used to ride shoulder-in itself, circles, serpentines, turns, corners, half-pass, pirouettes, canter depart and canter, counter-canter, flying changes and to correct faults in piaffe and passage.

The half-halt is used to assist the horse's balance, to improve his rhythm, to slow him down and to prepare him for each movement or change of instruction. Once learnt, it is used, in split-second timing, almost together with the forward instruction,* to develop engagement of the hindquarters, collection, lightness, the passage and the piaffe.

Before we are able to do a shoulder-in or a half-halt, we need to learn their building blocks. These building blocks enable us to develop coordination and light control.

The building blocks of the half-halt are the halt and the forward reaction. The building blocks of the shoulder-in are the bend on a straight line and the change

*Note A small time gap is always necessary to avoid giving two opposing messages. This timing is what is traditionally called, rider 'tact'.

of bend. The latter teaches riders to control the horse's shoulders. These building blocks also teach the horse the two basic commands – yield to rein pressure and yield to leg pressure. Without the half-halt and the ability to move on a straight line with a bend, horses cannot progress and riders cannot control the entire horse.

The early warning signal

Riding a horse has similarities to leading a blind person. The blind have to be warned before walking up steps or changing direction or they will resist or lose balance. The horse has no idea what the rider is going to ask of him at the next step unless he is prepared with clear, detailed and unambiguous explanations. If he is not prepared, he will lose balance or resist. An early warning signal gives the horse the opportunity to prepare his body for the changes of balance needed when changing direction, changing movements or transitions. This ensures better balance and smoother movements and transitions. Use soft feathering or rein vibrations to warn the horse before and during all directional changes and transitions. These vibrations tell the horse that he should not use his head and neck to balance.

STEP ONE – THE FORWARD RESPONSE

Step one is the forward response and step two is the halt response. For practical purposes step one and step two have to be taught together (although we will look at points pertinent to each separately). Although they may sound elementary, most riders do not communicate these simple requests correctly. If they are not performed correctly, the very important half-halts that derive from them will not be effective. To avoid giving opposing messages, the horse should not be in the 'on the bit' frame for these exercises.

The forward instruction is the building block of all forward riding. It includes transitions to extensions of the walk, trot and canter. It can be introduced and refined by work on a 20m circle:

- From halt, ask the horse to move off into walk by using the lightest possible lower leg (calf) pressure with both legs and ease the horse forwards. If he does not respond to light leg pressure, *do not* give another leg aid, but follow it up immediately with a whip tap or spur pressure. This tap should be strong enough to coerce him into taking an immediate step, but not so strong as to give him a fright. It should not be a punishment, but an encouragement. However, a tap which is too light will not have the desired effect and will habituate him to whip-tapping.

- As you give the leg pressure, yield your arms slightly forwards to allow the horse to move forwards. *This is extremely important.* It ensures that the reins do not cause mouth pressure during the forward command, thereby giving a simultaneous stopping instruction. Become very aware of your arms yielding because 99 per cent of riders pull back on the reins or tighten their arms as they ask the horse to move forwards. This is arguably the most important aspect of the forward instruction. Riders often complain that their horses do not move off the legs, are lazy or stubborn. This is generally caused by arm tightness. If you find it difficult to relax your arms, rest your hands on the horse's withers (see Chapters 10 and 11).

- Reward the horse by removing the pressure and relaxing (doing nothing) with your legs the instant he responds with a forward step.

- Walk a quarter or half circle and halt (see step two).

- After every halt, repeat this procedure of light calf pressure followed by a light whip tap and arm yielding until your coordination and timing are good and your horse reacts instantly.

below left The lower legs squeeze and the knees/adductors relax to ask for walk.

below right The knees squeeze and the lower legs relax for stopping.

STEP TWO – THE HALT RESPONSE

The halt response is a major building block in all riding. You can work on the halt response by using the 20m circle as in step one.

- Walk a quarter of the circle and ask your horse to halt. This halt need not be square because we teach one concept at a time.

- Vibrate or feather the reins lightly with alternate hands as an early warning signal. Keep your arms yielding while you squeeze the reins. This is the pre-aid which will eventually explain to the horse that he should remain 'on the bit' and the contact should remain yielding into the halt. It says, 'We are going to do a transition, please do not use your neck for balance by lifting it or pulling against the pressure.' At this stage, however, it serves to teach the rider fine motor co-ordination and to multi-task by adding more than one movement through the reins. Close your knees/thighs, but keep your lower legs clearly off the horse. The lower legs on the horse makes riders push inadvertently. This pushing, together with the closing knees, gives the horse two opposing messages – knee pressure to stop and calf pressure to go. Riders also learn far faster to coordinate knee pressure without simultaneous calf pressure. This is a temporary measure. Once riders have learnt not to push inadvertently with their calves, they will automatically fall passively against the horse's sides. Knee and calf pressure will eventually be used, *almost* simultaneously, when squaring up the horse's forelimbs (see Chapter 9).

I HAD INITIALLY BEEN taught to ask my horse to move forwards with my calves and to stop by holding him with both legs. (It had to be as though preventing a pencil, held in the fist, from falling through.) This method worked relatively well until I acquired a 4-year-old retired racehorse. Stopping was always prob-lematic, even as I worked up the levels. A new trainer taught me to close my knees to stop the horse, but did not tell me to remove my lower legs. This new 'aid' alleviated the problem, but stopping remained troublesome for years. The horse still seemed confused, so on one particularly difficult hack I decided to clarify the going and stopping aids by separating them completely. I removed my calves off his sides completely when using my knees/thighs and opened my knees when using my calves. It worked from the outset. I had, through trial and error, found a method which did not give the horse opposing messages and it solved my problem.

- If the horse does not respond by stopping immediately, you have to follow up the knee pressure immediately with stronger pressure. For stronger pressure, lock your elbows. This is not a pulling back, but a solid lock which prevents a forward step. Your arms and hands will go into co-contraction. This aid should be strong enough to convince the horse to stop immediately.

- As the horse halts, release all pressure immediately.

- Repeat these forward and stopping instructions until the horse is obedient to light calf pressure for moving off and only knee/thigh pressure for stopping. Horses learn extremely quickly that strong, uncomfortable mouth pressure follows the knee/thigh pressure. They hate bit pressure and try to avoid the discomfort. They thus learn to stop from only the knee/thigh pressure immediately after three to four repetitions. If it takes longer you are not doing it correctly. The horse must halt immediately. If you allow him to take three to five steps before halting, by not giving strong enough rein pressure, he will understand that your request is, 'Three to five steps before the halt' and you will thus teach him to give you three to five steps before halting. Therefore you have to be convincing in your request for an immediate halt. However, *if you do not release the pressure completely and instantly after his correct response,* he will try other incorrect methods of relieving the pressure. He may pull his head forwards or step back.

These exercises have to be repeated at least seven times correctly to develop the coordination and timing necessary to multi-task the aids of a) alternate hand/finger squeezing; b) knee pressure; c) elbow pressure and d) the release of all pressure. We can only learn correct coordination from correct repetition.

It is extremely important that there is a time space between the light pressure and the strong pressure. If the knee and hand pressure are simultaneous, the pressure-release system will not be successful. The horse will not understand that he should react to light pressure rather than wait for the strong pressure.

When your coordination is adequate, you can add back-bracing to the process. The sequence is then: vibrate your fingers; bring the lower edges of your shoulder blades tightly together like an 'angel's wingtips touching'. Follow up immediately with knee/thigh pressure and finally lock your elbows. Horses usually commence halting immediately off the bracing contraction of the muscles between the lower edges of your shoulder blades. Chapter 8 explains this in detail.

When you do this, do not lean back. This action causes a forward-pushing feel on the horse's back which he interprets as a forward command. In contrast, bracing the back by bringing the lower borders of your shoulder blades together automatically deepens your seat. When the horse moves forwards off light pressure and halts off knee pressure alone, both rider and horse are ready for step three.

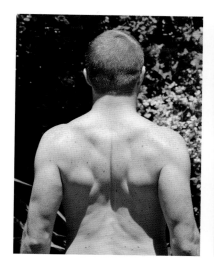 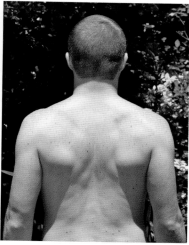

far left The instruction to 'straighten the shoulders' causes shoulder elevation, back hollowing and general tightness.

left Bracing the back is contracting the rhomboid muscles (see page 141) by bringing the shoulder blade wingtips together. It straightens and drops the shoulders, stretching the spine up.

STEP THREE – THE SIDEWAYS RESPONSE OF THE HINDQUARTERS

The turn on the forehand – the first leg-yielding exercise

The turn on the forehand is the easiest lateral movement for both horse and rider. It is the cornerstone of all lateral movements and also pirouettes, insofar as the latter need strong leg pressure to keep the hind legs in place. It teaches the horse to move away from single leg pressure – the sideways response – and gives riders control of the horse's hindquarters. It should be taught to young horses within the first week of training because it gives so much more control. This exercise is important for all riders. It teaches riders individual leg coordination and effective body use. They learn to dissociate the leg adductor muscles and use each leg independently. They also learn to dissociate the movements of their arms and legs and thus not to pull with the arm on the side of the pushing leg. By preventing the hand from pulling, the leg coordination and effectiveness automatically develop faster. Correctly executed, it gives riders total lateral control of the horse's haunches. The exercise can be performed as follows.

- Halt on the track on the long side of the arena.

- Hold both reins with equal light contact throughout the movement. Your hands should be used only to prevent forward movement and to avoid reinforcing backward movement. Neither hand should pull backwards. It is best to touch your knuckles together or link your thumbs to avoid inadvertently pulling on one rein, especially the left rein (see Chapter 3). The hind leg movement should not be the result of a reaction from the inside hand, but rather a yielding to leg pressure alone.

> **THE TRADITIONAL METHOD** of riding the turn on the forehand is to pull with the rein on the same side as the pushing leg. Although this encourages the horse to move his hindquarters sideways through the automatic equine neck reaction (ENR) which tightens the neck and the spine, moving the hindquarters out, it defeats the object of leg-yielding. Instead it teaches the horse to move off the hand and not off the leg.

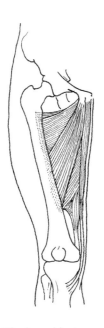

The leg adductors.

- Take your outside leg off the horse to dissociate the action of the adductor muscles of one leg from the other. This teaches the adductors of the two legs to work independently.

  The human body automatically tends to use the adductors of both legs simultaneously. In leg-yield exercises this gives the horse opposing messages. Removing the outside leg pressure altogether prevents confusion and tension in the horse. It is a temporary measure which may look odd. However, it teaches the rider's body to coordinate pushing with one leg while the other leg remains passive. This method speeds up rider coordination when learning the new movement pattern. When your coordination and body use have developed sufficiently to dissociate the movement of your legs and you have learnt to use them independently, this leg will automatically return and rest passively against the horse's side. If the horse does not step sideways, you are most probably pushing with both legs, giving opposing messages. Most novice riders have difficulty in using their legs independently. By learning this exercise early in training, riders learn to multi-task from the onset of riding.

- Place your inside leg further back onto the horse's belly. Push the horse's hindquarters over with this leg. Ideally you should use light pressure followed by a light tap with the whip, or spur pressure. Initially you may need very strong leg pressure because the horse may not understand that he has to move sideways. If you are a novice rider, your leg strength and coordination may not be sufficiently developed to convince the horse. The sensation of the push may initially feel stronger if your muscles are weak. Push as though pushing *through* the horse, then follow with light whip tapping. Push the horse until he takes one sideways step. Remove the pressure immediately and reward him with a tickle on the neck. Continue to ask for one sideways step at a time with a reward after each step. Continuous pushing after the horse has taken the step will not reward him for the correct response.

He may also move over too fast in fright. Besides, continuous pushing will render your leg useless. When the horse understands this pressure, it should be lightened to the lightest aid you would like to give, followed by a tap of the whip.

If your leg pressure and tapping has no effect, your trainer can push against your leg until the horse takes a step. Three repetitions are all that is needed for the horse to understand that he is to move away from this pressure. Horses generally respond more readily when asked to move in one direction than the other when learning the turn on the forehand: it evens out in about two lessons.

 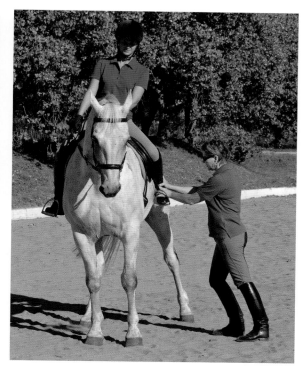

TEACHING **THE HORSE** the turn on the forehand through groundwork first, may speed up the process. However, one of the major purposes of teaching the turn on the forehand is to develop rider coordination, muscle strength and timing.

• Do not allow forward stepping as this teaches the horse to evade sideways stepping. The first sign of the horse moving forwards will be his shoulders leaning forwards. As you feel this, move your arms back or lock your elbows. Release as he begins to stop this slight leaning. If you allow him to take a forward step, he will assume that you want him to do so and he will take longer to learn to step sideways.

above left The turn on the forehand with the inside leg pushing and the outside leg off the horse. There is no pull on the reins.

above right The trainer can push against the pupil's leg to give the feeling of the amount of pressure needed for the horse to understand that he is required to yield.

- Backward stepping is common and acceptable at this stage because it does not evade the sideways stepping. Should the horse step back, do not urge him forwards with your legs, but immediately soften the contact by pushing both arms forwards to make loops in the reins. Maintain this loose contact until he stops stepping back. However, you have to continue pushing him sideways with your one leg, throughout his backward steps. He will eventually reach the track with continuous sideways steps even though he is also moving backwards. Horses learn very quickly that they cannot evade the sideways stepping by moving backwards and thus give up this evasion within three repetitions provided the rider's body use is correct and the reins are properly yielded. Backward pressure on the horse's mouth will give him a backward-stepping aid.

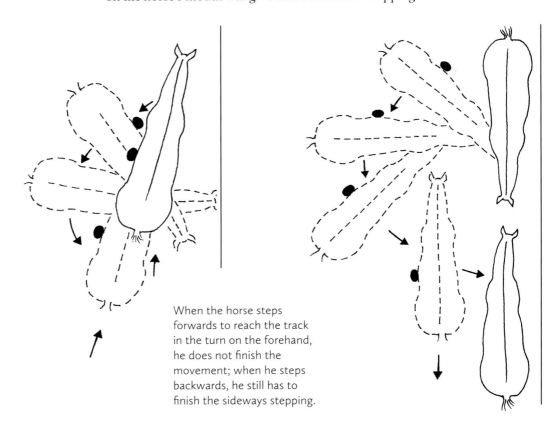

When the horse steps forwards to reach the track in the turn on the forehand, he does not finish the movement; when he steps backwards, he still has to finish the sideways stepping.

- Walk forwards for about 10–15m. Change your whip and repeat the exercise on the other rein.

- Should the horse move his shoulder sideways, move both hands to the opposite side to control his shoulders. The outside rein, against his shoulder, will prevent him from stepping sideways.

- Your arms thus move back when the horse steps forwards. They move forwards when the horse steps back. They move left when the horse's shoulders push right and they move to the right when the horse's shoulders move to the left. Throughout, your hands should be close together to move as one.

- Repeat this exercise until you can perform it with ease and without any pull on the reins. Sleep on it and repeat it the next day. It should then be an entrenched new pattern of movement for both you and the horse, and you will have learnt better body use. Once easy to perform, there will be no need to practise this movement ever again because it is only a training movement.

above left Soften the reins when the horse starts to lean, or walks, backwards.

above right Tighten the reins when the horse starts to lean, or walks, forwards.

STEP FOUR – CHANGING BEND ON A STRAIGHT LINE; CONTROLLING THE SHOULDERS

When riders can perform the first three steps with ease, they should be ready for the most important basic exercise in their quest to be fully effective. It teaches immediate effectiveness and control of the horse's shoulders.

Bending while moving in a straight line is another foundation building block of manège work. It is the most important balance exercise for horses to learn because it is biomechanically opposite to their natural method of turning (see Author's Note). This is the bent-straight position. This exercise reinforces the use of the inside rein to bend the horse's neck and the outside rein to move the horse's shoulders. It also teaches the rider not to give opposing leg aids, thus giving the rider a far greater understanding of the aids. It is a major step in learning to multi-task.

Preparatory concepts

Head and shoulder movement

Humans turn with rotation. They start the turn by rotating their necks; this is followed by shoulder rotation, then the hips and finally the feet turn, all in quick succession. In nature, rigid-backed quadrupeds, such as horses, turn and move on curves by taking sideways steps with their forelegs and move their heads and necks to the opposite side in counterbalance: they 'fall in' (see photo on page 23 in Chapter 2). Dressage and jumping horses are required to turn with bend to maintain control of their shoulders to ensure the specific balance required for this work. They thus bend their necks in the direction of the turn – the inside, then turn by taking their natural sideways steps.

This change from the horse's natural method of turning changes his centre of gravity. During an inside bend he has to place more weight on his outside legs to maintain balance in turns and circles. Therefore, the rider has to control the horse's shoulders during the turn. The bent-straight position teaches the rider to do this with the outside rein and to bend him with the inside leg and rein. It also teaches control of the horse's ribcage and is the basis of developing suppleness, straightness and the start of engagement. Flexibility is needed to bend in balance and bend is needed to become flexible.

The horse's ribcage hangs loose between his shoulder blades because horses do not have collarbones; the ribcage can therefore swing from side to side. This idiosyncrasy helps the rider to move the horse's centre of gravity sideways when asking for bend. You can read more about this and other biomechanical idiosyncrasies in *Equine Biomechanics for Riders – The Key to Balanced Riding*.

Turning the horse's head

The inside rein turns, through vibrations, only the horse's head, points his nose in the direction of the turn and bends his neck. (It *can* turn the horse if you pull the rein, but the bend will be false because the horse's head and neck are pulled

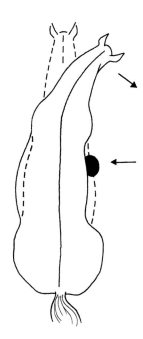

left Humans turn with rotation.

right The dressage horse turns with bend.

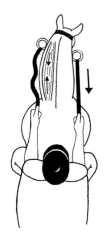

above When the rider pulls the inside rein to turn, the horse pulls against this pressure and is using his outside neck muscles. The outside rein is softer than the inside.

into the turn. The horse pulls against this force, thus using his opposite – outside – neck muscles.) The inside rein is not effective in dictating the size of circles: it can make a circle smaller (usually at the expense of turning it into a spiral and interfering with forward movement), but it cannot enlarge the circle. The bending aid should thus not *steer* the horse in circles, turns, or serpentines, or seek to control the angle of the shoulder-in and half-pass.

To gain a better picture of what is, and is not required, do the following exercise. At halt, ask your horse to bend his own neck by sponging or vibrating the rein. Release the pressure when the horse bends his neck. There should be no pulling to make him bend. If your horse moves his shoulders from your inside rein pressure, he has tightened his neck muscles against your pull. When the horse bends his neck only, his shoulders do not move. This shows that we bend the horse with a sponging inside rein (together with a pushing inside leg).

Moving the horse's shoulders

The outside rein moves the horse's shoulders and turns him. It is the outside rein which dictates the size of the circles. Try the following exercises:

1. While mounted at the halt, move your horse's shoulders half a metre to the left using only your reins, no legs. As you are moving his shoulders, analyse which

of your reins is most effective at moving him sideways. Move your horse's shoulders back to the right to their original position using only the reins. You will feel that your opening inside rein initiates the movement, but the outside rein is more effective at moving the horse's shoulders. If you are not sure which rein did the job, take both reins in one hand and repeat the exercise. You will notice that the outside rein, against the horse's shoulders, is the more active and effective rein. You may have to cross the withers with your outside rein to convince the horse to move (see Chapter 11).

2. Walk a circle. Open your outside rein to enlarge the circle. When your circle is large, make it smaller again by closing your outside rein against the horse's shoulder.

right Open the outside rein to enlarge the circle.

far right Close the outside rein to reduce the circle.

Changing the bend

The following exercise is started in walk as you approach the short side of the arena, but you will be riding up the centre line for the main part of this exercise.

• As you approach the corner, push the horse's ribcage over with your inside leg to elicit an inside bend. Take your outside leg off to avoid giving opposing messages.

- Open your outside rein to control the horse's shoulders and prevent them from 'falling in' or turning too soon. Do not vibrate it.

- Vibrate or sponge the inside rein to explain to the horse to bend (turn) his head and neck. *Do not* pull the head and neck into the bend. Release the pressure as he yields to bend. The inside rein will be soft when the horse is using his own inside neck muscles to bend. If there is tension on this rein, your pressure-release is not correct. The horse may appear to be bending, but is tightening his outside neck muscles in a false bend. All the rein techniques are described in Chapter 11.

- When the horse yields to inside rein pressure, move your outside rein towards his shoulder in the direction of your inside hip. This turns his shoulders up the centre line while you continue to vibrate the inside rein throughout the turn to maintain a soft bend. Vibrating with the inside rein while the outside rein moves the horse's shoulders teaches your hands and arms to multi-task.

- Walk straight up the centre line. You now have to learn to walk on a straight line and change the bend before changing the direction. Open the new outside rein to hold the horse's shoulders on the straight line.

- Change the pushing leg. Push the ribcage over with the new inside leg and remove the other leg off the horse.

- Vibrate/sponge the new inside rein to ask the horse for the new bend – see drawings and photos overleaf.

- Continue to walk straight up the centre line using your opening outside rein and pushing inside leg to prevent the horse from turning (falling on his shoulder) and maintain the vibrations/feathering until the horse maintains the bend. You will be ready to turn when you can walk straight with the horse bending his own neck to the inside (you will know this from the soft feeling on the inside rein and the horse's ability to continue walking straight up the centre line).

- When you are ready to turn (the precise distance you have ridden down the centre line, is not the issue – it is the readiness to turn) continue with small vibrations/feathering on the inside rein as you move your outside hand and rein closer to the horse's shoulder to turn him towards the long side. Maintain the new inside leg pressure. Continue to vibrate on the inside rein as you walk to the track while controlling the size of the turn with a straight and firm opening or closing outside rein and pushing inside leg until you reach the track. Your outside leg remains 'off' the horse. Walk straight up the track towards the corner into the short side. You will now be on the other rein.

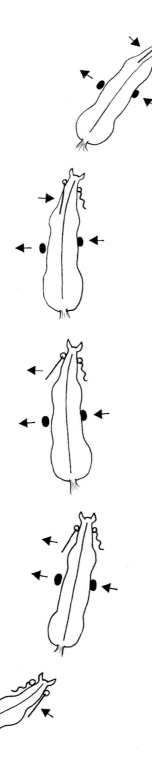

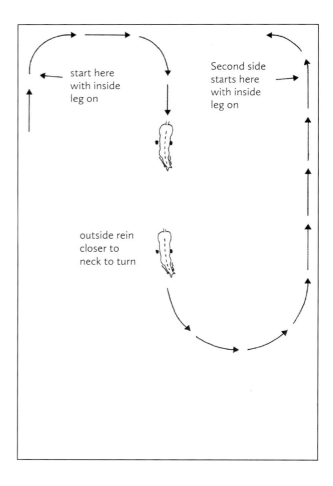

left and below The phases of changing the bend down the centre line. The small diagram shows relative positioning within the arena.

start here
with inside
leg on

Second side
starts here
with inside
leg on

outside rein
closer to
neck to turn

- Before the corner onto the short side, push the horse's ribcage over with your inside leg, vibrate the inside rein and, when the horse yields to the inside, turn him up the centre line again by bringing your outside rein closer to his shoulders.

- Change the bend up the centre line as described above and, when the horse yields to the new inside bend and you can maintain him walking straight, turn him with the new outside rein.

- Repeat until you are able to vibrate with one hand and control the horse's shoulders with the other, can push the ribcage with one leg while the other is completely passive and can walk straight with a bend without the horse 'falling in'.

The important part of this exercise is the change of bend without the change of direction. Although it may sound too complicated, most novices and beginners from the age of 10 understand immediately. All learn the coordination necessary for this exercise after a few attempts.

The change of bend.

above left Walking straight with a right bend. Note the soft vibrating right rein, right leg pressure, shoulder-controlling left rein and the left leg off the horse.

above centre The change of bend, with changing leg and arm aids and the horse walking straight.

above right The new left bend, with the horse starting the turn.

THIS IS AN EXERCISE in which each of the rider's limbs does a different movement. The inside hand has to continue vibrating throughout each bend and turn. The outside hand may only move the shoulders once the horse has bent his own neck. The inside leg on the girth pushes the ribcage while the outside leg is passive off the horse. This is true multi-tasking which the body usually takes 24 hours to integrate. The brain practises and consolidates new coordination skills while we sleep. You may struggle to get the coordination on the first day, but after a good night's sleep, it will be easy the next day.

At this stage of learning body use, the outside leg is not involved in turning. Once the movement of both legs have been dissociated, the outside leg should be added, in a slightly drawn back position, to move the hindquarters and assist turning, especially in tight circles and turns. This usually happens automatically when you learn the walk pirouette.

This exercise teaches both horse and rider the correct inside bend, which is the basis of the concept of 'riding from the inside leg to the outside rein'. Initially the 'take and give' of the inside rein together with the pushing inside leg is necessary. Eventually the horse will learn to change his weight through the bend. He will develop enough stretch on the outside, strength on the inside and knowledge of the concept to maintain the inside bend almost on his own. The inside hand will have a feeling of yielding; a soft rein. The outside rein contact will be more positive. The bend will be maintained with the inside leg alone and the horse will change bend as the new inside leg starts to push. During a serpentine the trained horse will change his bend as the rider starts to push with the new inside leg.

When you can perform the previous four exercises, you will have control over the horse's head and neck, his shoulders, his ribcage and his hindquarters.

NATURAL OUTCOMES

These four steps have a few automatic natural outcomes which enhance riding.

The round flexor frame

The round flexor frame is the 'on the bit' frame which ensures that the horse uses his correct flexor muscles for athletic development. This position changes the horse from a caterpillar into a butterfly. He becomes light, submissive, pliable, forward and focused. When, however, his back muscles (trunk extensors) contract, his neck hollows and his back and hips straighten in extension. This leads to the opposite of engagement. See *Equine Biomechanics for Riders – The Key to Balanced Riding* if you wish to read more on the subject.

All young horses, and horses with unspoiled mouths, automatically start to round in a flexor frame when these exercises are performed correctly. The vibrating pressure and bending lead to soft yielding contact provided the pressure is released completely the moment the horse yields. Horses learn quickly that it is

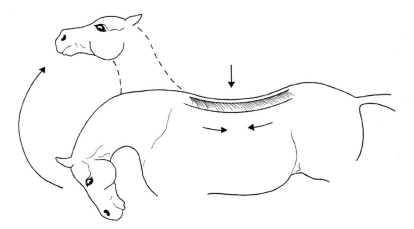

The horse's extensor muscles start contracting when he begins to move his head and neck from the fully flexed position. They continue to contract until the horse's head, neck and back are fully extended in a hollow frame.

far more comfortable to yield to rein pressure in a round flexor frame than to have the bit cause constant pressure in the mouth. However, horses who have developed defensive mouth behaviour, or have damaged mouth nerves from consistent strong contact, may need to learn the concept of yielding with stronger pressure. This is explained in Chapter 11.

RELAXED AND YIELDING arms, shoulders, elbows and wrists are prerequisites for the flexor frame. An elastic contact is essential. If you do not have an independent seat or your arms are not relaxed, you will have to ride with loose reins. Only take up a light contact once you have learnt not to inadvertently interfere with the horse's mouth.

Rider position

The four steps improve rider coordination and body use. Correct body use automatically produces correct body position. Riders do not have to contort and become rigid to achieve a good position when they become well coordinated and can multi-task, because form follows function.

Horse anxiety

The horses' anxiety disappears. Consistent delivery of the requests allows horses to predict the correct responses. The disposal of conflicting instructions removes the horse's anxiety because he understands the requests and knows how to respond correctly. His whole demeanour changes to calmness, confidence and ease of movement. His neck drops, his eyes become soft ('doe-eyed') and his mouth becomes more relaxed.

The canter

Once you and your horse can perform these changes of bend at the trot, you can start to canter. His canter will immediately be easier, slower and more balanced. He will move in a round flexor frame when you squeeze the reins. He will slow down, develop rhythm and maintain the circle.

> A NOVICE RIDER MAY not be able to penetrate through the resistances of a horse with defensive mouth behaviour. The trainer should correct the horse first. Once the horse understands yielding to rein pressure, novice riders will be able to feel the correct kinaesthetic and tactile sensations and learn faster. If the trainer is not able to ride or correct the horse, the rider should be given the opportunity to feel the sensations on a correctly schooled horse.

You and your horse will now possess the coordination and understand all the basic concepts necessary to get you to the top level of dressage and jumping. Your training programme should now continue along the six-step athletic training format which is generally referred to as *The Scales of Training*.

> I USE THIS FOUR-STEP programme for all riders from beginners, through novice riders up to Advanced level, should the latter have problems. Advanced level riders usually move through the four steps in one lesson, after which their problems are easier to solve.

ADDITIONAL EXERCISES

Once riders can do the four steps with coordination and ease, they can add these additional exercises. They are variations on the theme which consolidate and refine the four steps.

Activating the walk and refining the aid

- Once walking, ask the horse to be more active with alternate light calf pressure. This should not be continuous. Give light left and then right calf pressure and if he does not react instantly, follow with a whip tap. Relax your legs until the horse's first step of slowing down. Immediately give light alternate leg pressure followed by a whip tap. Then do nothing again until the next slowing down. After three correct repetitions, your horse's walk should continue to be active.

- Transfer your leg aids to seat aids for walk. Use alternate light pressure from alternate lower legs together with alternate hamstring contraction of the seat. The leg and seat on the same side should contract together. The horse will associate the calf pressure with the hamstring pressure. (How to contract the hamstrings of each leg independently is explained in Chapter 8.)

- Use alternate hamstring seat muscle contraction without the calf pressure. Your calf pressure can now be used as the stronger pressure to activate the walk should the horse become dull to your hamstring contractions. Horses respond to seat pressure by giving longer steps.

Alternating long steps and short steps at the walk to refine the walk

This exercise:

- Teaches riders more control.
- Gives beginners the confidence that they can control the speed of the horse.
- Makes the horse more sensitive to the aids.
- Makes the horse more obedient.
- Improves the horse's movement through alternating the level of engagement.

To perform the exercise:

- Ask your horse to give longer steps by moving your arms slightly forwards, allowing your hips to move more forwards and back and by giving alternate seat (hamstring) aids. Stronger calf aids usually speed up and shorten the walk steps. Take these longer steps for about five to ten strides.

- Shorten the walk steps by taking your arms back a little, vibrating the reins and closing your knees without halting. In other words, a half-halt without calf pressure. Release the pressure on your reins as the horse takes the shorter steps. There should be no rein pressure while he is taking short steps unless he speeds up, in which case you should half-halt again. Shorten the steps as much as possible.

- Alternate the short and the longer steps around the arena until you and your horse can do this with ease and without you holding him in with the reins.

The figure-of-eight at trot

The figure-of-eight at trot is the same concept as the change of bend exercise at walk. It is based on two 20m circles which are connected by a straight line that runs between the quarter lines of the arena (see illustration). The exercise reinforces the rider's control of the horse's shoulders. The faster speed of the movement further develops rider coordination, reaction time and multi-tasking.

- Ride the main, circular portion of the exercise as though on two 20m circles (as in a figure-of-eight) but, as you approach the first quarter line, ride in a straight line between this and the far quarter line during the change of bend. The point of the exercise is to trot in a straight line while changing the bend.

- When you reach the first quarter line, ride a half-halt to slow the horse down, prepare him for the change and help him to balance through the change.

- Open your new outside rein to control the horse's shoulders and prevent him from turning.

- Simultaneously, push the horse's ribcage with your new inside leg while removing your new outside leg.

- Sponge/vibrate your new inside rein until the horse yields to it by bending his neck in the new direction. He must continue to move straight until he yields to this new bend.

- At the second quarter line, close your outside rein towards the horse's shoulder and move his shoulders into the turn while you continue to vibrate your inside rein.

Figure-of-eight change of bend.

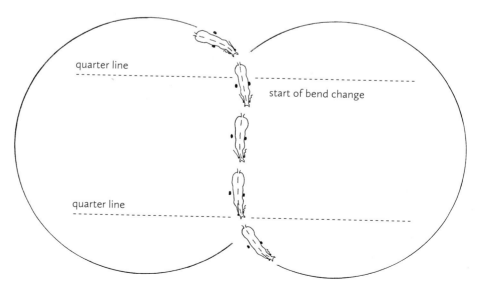

quarter line

start of bend change

quarter line

- Continue onto the new 20m circle and repeat the process in the other direction.

- Continue with the exercise until your horse stops 'falling in' on all the turns.

If your inside leg is ineffective, imagine pushing the horse out in leg-yield; your leg will become more effective. If the horse keeps 'falling in', step out with your outside leg as you are pushing his ribcage with your inside leg as described in Chapter 9. This stops the 'falling in' immediately.

Leg-yielding

When horse and rider understand and have developed the appropriate coordination through the turn on the forehand and changes of bend, it should be relatively easy to learn to leg-yield. This movement does not disturb the horse's natural balance. In leg-yielding the horse moves laterally, crossing his legs. He is bent slightly away from the direction of the movement. The bend, the direction and impulsion are all controlled by the rider's inside leg, while the outside leg is passive. It can be taught early in the training of both horse and rider because the multi-tasking is simple. The leg-yield is taught best with the horse's head towards the wall.

Leg-yielding improves the ability of the horse to move in straight lines, to stay on the track and to maintain the correct-sized circles because the rider learns better control of the horse's shoulders. It also affords the following benefits:

- It improves leg use by strengthening the rider's legs and consolidating the co-ordination of moving one leg while the other remains inactive.

- Better horse control improves rider confidence.

- It reinforces the horse's concept of moving away from lateral leg pressure and thus corrects 'falling in', bend problems and even the canter depart.

- It is an excellent schooling exercise for flexibility and even engagement in all gaits.

- Most importantly, it teaches the rider more about communication with the horse and how the outside rein controls the horse's shoulders.

Leg-yielding with the horse's head to the wall

In leg-yielding your *outside* arm and leg are on the side *to which the horse is moving* and your *inside* arm and leg are on the side *away from* the direction of movement.

- Walk the horse around the short side of the arena. Turn down the quarter line, but point the horse's head and shoulders at a 45-degree angle to the wall. You will be pushing the horse up the long side of the arena.

- Maintain the angle while you push the horse's hindquarters sideways with your inside leg well behind the girth. (Your leg position will become more centred once the leg-yield is easy). Push and release at every stride to ensure that the horse does not habituate to the pressure, but do not remove your leg. Keep your other leg off the horse to prevent confusion and to develop your coordination of pushing with one leg only.

- The hands are decisive in this exercise. Keep them close together, preferably with the knuckles touching each other, or by holding one thumb with the other hand, and use them together.

- The outside hand controls the shoulder angle. When the horse's hindquarters start to move too close to the track, thus losing the angle, move your outside hand towards the horse's shoulders and in the direction of your inside hip (Thus in, and back). The outside hand straightens the horse's spine, moving the hindquarters in line with the neck. It stops the shoulder from 'popping out' and negates the necessity to push harder with your inside leg.

- If the angle becomes too big, the horse will not be able to cross his legs. Open your outside hand a fraction to move his shoulders over and close the angle to the wall. Your rein movements should be fairly small, or the horse's adjustments will be too large and you will have to readjust again.

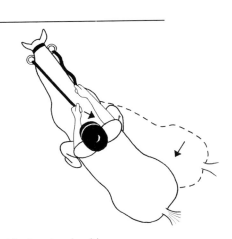

Moving the shoulders to increase the angle.

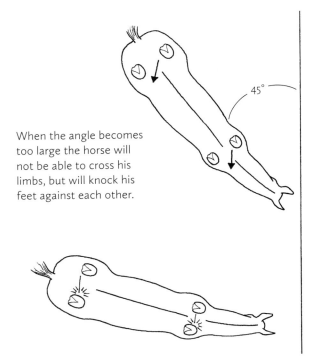

When the angle becomes too large the horse will not be able to cross his limbs, but will knock his feet against each other.

- Continue with the inside leg pressure and adjusting the angle with both hands together as a unit until the angle becomes consistent.

- If the horse takes backward steps, release all rein pressure by moving both hands forwards, but continue with the leg pressure.

- If the horse moves forwards towards the wall, ride a two-handed half-halt using convincing pressure. Release as the horse stops pulling forwards.

- When your angle is fairly consistent and the horse does not pull forwards you can add the round flexor frame through rein vibrations.

Changing bend and preventing the horse's shoulders from 'falling in' or out becomes much easier once you have mastered this exercise.

Tips for leg-yielding

- You will be more effective with your feet out of the stirrups.

- Any tightness in your body will block forward movement. If the horse stops moving, check for tension in your body.

- Start the exercise on the quarter line because the horse inevitably moves forwards toward the wall (or fence). The wall helps riders to control the forward movement and it compels the horse to yield and step sideways instead of evading the sideways steps by moving forwards. Both horse and rider develop coordination faster because 'cheating' is noticed immediately. Riders thus have to be more effective. The leg-yield from the centre line across the diagonal is a good exercise for the young horse, but unfortunately it lulls riders into a false sense of effectiveness. Riders have to imagine the wall diagonally across the arena and have to maintain the horse's nose on this imaginary line. Therefore neither riders nor trainers may notice that the horse actually moves mainly forwards and barely sideways because the quality of the sideways steps is difficult to judge without a wall. The absence of a wall prevents riders from learning control of the horse's shoulders. The shoulders usually 'fall out' and the hind legs trail. This method takes longer to get the message across to both horse and rider because the rider's aids are not precise enough.

- If your half-halts are not effective enough to prevent the horse from moving too close to the wall, imagine leg-yielding on a line across the diagonal of the arena. Your leg and body will automatically push the horse away from the wall. Once away, push parallel to the wall again – see diagrams overleaf.

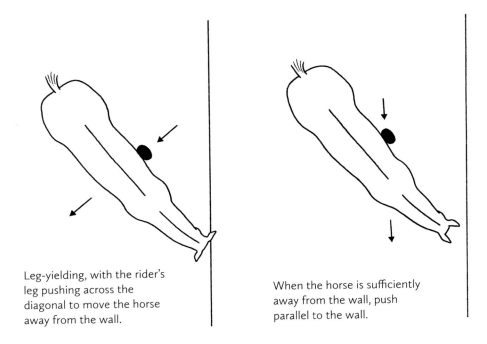

Leg-yielding, with the rider's leg pushing across the diagonal to move the horse away from the wall.

When the horse is sufficiently away from the wall, push parallel to the wall.

- If the horse does not react sufficiently to your outside hand moving closer to his shoulder, you can cross the withers with your outside hand towards your inside hip. The rein should not be floppy. This encourages the horse to move his shoulders over and increase the angle with his hindquarters. It is important that horses react correctly to our aids, or they learn incorrectly. It is the inside hand that should not cross the withers to move the shoulders because it only bends the horse's neck; it does not move the shoulders (see Chapter 11). The horse will soon respond from light movement of your outside hand towards his shoulders and you will never have to cross the withers again.

- Assess the angle of the movement with visual feedback to see whether the hind-quarters are leading or trailing. Compare the sharp angle between your horse and the wall by looking over your inside shoulder. Your outside hand and your inside leg will automatically adjust to correct the angle through your visual motor coordination. Looking at the outside angle is not effective.

Chapter 8

|||||||||||||||||||||||||||||||||||||||||||||||||||||||||||||||||||||||||||||||||||||||||||||||||||||||||||||||||||||||||||||||||||||||||||||||||||||||||||||||||||||||||||

BIOMECHANICS OF THE SEAT AND WEIGHT AIDS

ALTHOUGH BODY USE in the form of the weight, leg and rein aids is discussed separately in this and the following three chapters, these aids are generally used in a 'symphony of aids'. All the body parts contribute to the whole conversation with the horse.

One of the most difficult concepts for novice riders to grasp is the weight aid. Novices generally attempt to change weight influences by leaning. The leaning action alone has little effect on the horse (or even an opposite effect from that expected) unless he is trained to react to it.* The rider leaning to one side may lead to the horse's shoulder 'falling in' to the same side while his head moves to the other side in counterbalance. However, it can also have no effect. This is evident when horses turn towards other horses, towards the stable, or when running out of a jump while the novice rider is desperately pulling the opposite rein and leaning to the opposite side as the horse's shoulder continues to move in his preferred direction.

The seat and weight aids, to all intents and purposes, are the same, because the horse perceives all seat and weight aids as changes of pressure.

*Note I have written extensively on the biomechanical effect of the rider's weight and position on the horse's balance in my other books. In this chapter the effect of weight changes for communication and learning is discussed.

PRINCIPLES OF THE WEIGHT AIDS

Riders communicate all the weight aids through their bases of support – seat and hips. Horses perceive weight changes as deep pressure changes in their skin and muscles. They feel weight shifts as well as changes in quality of pressure through the saddle, although they perceive this only *during* the changes of pressure on their backs. Horses habituate quickly to constant pressure, so all weight aids have to be given in a pressure-release manner because sustained pressure does not constitute an aid.

Weight is changed through movement; movement is changed through muscle action – all our weight changes are caused by the contractions and relaxation of different muscle groups or body parts. Whenever a rider moves, the weight and deep pressure location on the horse's back changes. Pushing out the stomach below the belly button or bloating the stomach wall is a weight change which deepens the seat. Sitting deeper is produced by hip flexion. A rider can change the pressure on their horse's back by manoeuvring their weight from one part to another. When riders know which muscle groups to contract, they will know how to shift their weight.

We can place our weight in any direction on the saddle: slightly forward as in rein-back; slightly back when pushing the horse forwards. We can move it more to one side or to the other for changes of bend and for the canter position. We can move it at any angle for specific lateral movements. We can also 'lighten' the seat by stretching the spine up. We can deepen it by 'smiling' with our 'sitting cheeks' and pushing out the belly button.

Riders themselves feel weight changes from the horse through the saddle. The horse's weight shift is very noticeable when his shoulder 'falls' into or out of the circle or when he is carrying too much weight on his forehand. A lame horse places more weight on his sound leg to lighten the burden of the painful leg. Riders can feel this as a harder thump on one buttock. Not all riders are equally sensitive to these weight changes in the horse. Some feel the change immediately while others seem to be blissfully unaware.

Another type of weight aid is one that affects the horse's equilibrium. He then has to change his posture to adapt to the aid. We can thus 'throw' him off balance. For example, when a horse has an entrenched counter-canter and is resistant to learning flying changes by the more refined methods, we can teach him the concept by challenging his balance reactions. We disturb his weight with a sudden change in direction: he has no choice but to change lead. It need only be repeated once or twice until he understands the concept, after which any of the many other preferred methods should be used, depending on the need of the horse and rider. There seems to be a common fear that horses may learn to swing their hindquarters if taught by this method, but horses only swing their quarters because of the ENR when they do not yield in the neck. If the neck is pliable before and during the changes, the hindquarters do not swing and the changes are generally clean.

Meaningful and meaningless weight changes

Although horses feel every weight change or movement on their backs, not all weight changes necessarily lead to a response. Horses perceive all the rider's trunk and seat movements as either *incidental weight changes* or as *specific weight aids*. The former, incidental weight change is a meaningless seat correction, postural fault, salute in a dressage test, or a random movement. The specific weight aid is a meaningful form of communication, to which horses learn to respond. Horses are excellent at picking up cues: they learn, very quickly, to differentiate between meaningful communicating weight changes, to which they must react, and random, meaningless weight changes and movements, which they should ignore. However, they do so only after a process of clear 'explanations' and the correct pressure-release system of training: through repetition the weight influence becomes a 'signal'.

Meaningless weight changes are incidental changes, which have little effect on the horse's balance. They do not have a cause-effect influence on communication because there is no pressure-release-reward involved. A weight aid is more than simply having your weight in the wrong place. Leaning too far forwards, backwards or collapsing in the waist does not constitute a weight aid. Horses have to understand the change of weight, or the change has to elicit a balance reaction in the horse, for it to become a meaningful communication aid. It is interesting to note that horses adapt with ease to a rider with scoliosis who cannot sit straight and to polo players who move constantly. This is because they have learnt that these weight changes are meaningless background movements and not rider-horse communication. When riders have positional and postural deficiencies, their bodies automatically rearrange themselves into balance around their centres of gravity. The crookedness is thus imperceptible to the horse (see photos page 42).

WHEN A YOUNG HORSE learns to counter-canter he will often do a flying change when changing direction or when his balance is disturbed. Continuous correct counter-canter is an unnatural movement for the horse. However, it is often difficult to teach a horse with an entrenched counter-canter to understand that he should do a flying change, even through large balance disturbances. Such horses may continue in counter-canter despite repeated attempts at coercing a change through large weight displacements and positioning.

Figure-ground perception in weight aids

Figure-ground perception is the ability to distinguish foreground objects, movements or sounds from background objects, movements or sounds. It plays an important role in communicating with the horse. When we have a discussion with another person, that person and their words are the foreground on which we focus. All other objects and sounds, such as barking dogs, become the background, which we learn to ignore. The horse learns to distinguish between the foreground movements – meaningful weight changes (the aids), and the meaningless background movements and weight changes such as sneezes or adjustments of the stirrups, girth, clothes and position. The latter he ignores. He will simply adjust to them and it will have little effect on his balance and movement in general.

If horses reacted to all our weight changes simply because the changes affected their balance, we would have so many reactions from them as to make it almost impossible to ride.

Polo ponies cope with extreme weight changes, yet understand the requirement to continue to canter straight. If they turned every time the rider leaned over to hit the ball, the ball would never be hit. The vaulting horse never loses rhythm or balance no matter who is vaulting on him or where the rider sits, stands or leans. We have all seen a showjumping rider losing a stirrup and their balance before the last fence: they hold on for dear life, clear the fence, then let go and fall on the other side of the finish line. The horse simply continues because his balance is so superior. Advanced dressage horses are so well schooled that they ignore beginner riders' clumsy movements and aids. They react to correct body use.

Misconceived weight aids

Novice riders often do not understand the feel of a specific aid. All too often the aids are explained in terminology which is foreign to them. The weight aids are the most mysterious of all.

It is difficult to understand how to manoeuvre one's weight onto one foot or one hip. Leaning does not necessarily affect the horse's perception. The rider's body makes an automatic balance adjustment, rearranging itself around its centre of gravity over its base of support (the seat or feet). The rider's waist bulges to the other side; the rider's gravity line maintains the same position on the horse with a new arrangement around it (see photo on page 42 in Chapter 3) If riders lean over without making this automatic adjustment, they may fall if the horse turns in the other direction. Leaning over is not a weight aid.

'Stepping into the stirrup' is another esoteric phrase and not as simple as it sounds. When the instruction is given to put weight into a particular foot, riders have to figure out how to do this. First they will step on the stirrup with the ball of the foot. They do this by tightening the quadriceps muscle. This straightens the knee and hip and pushes down onto the ball of the foot. It generally lifts the rider's hip and weight off the seat and is the opposite from what was intended. Instead of placing more weight on the seat bone, it lightens the seat bone. It is not the stirrup which has to be weighted, but the seat bone.

Weight/seat aid exercises

To achieve weighting the seat bone, you have to lift your opposite hip. This automatically drops weight onto your appropriate seat bone, leg and foot. It gives the correct feel of dropping weight into the stirrup. The movement may be large at first because of inadequate coordination, but it will eventually become invisible.

Lift your hip to drop your opposite hip and foot in the stirrup.

Dismounted body awareness exercises

The following dismounted exercises teach you to shift your bodyweight. Practise these exercises for a few days. Performing them when mounted will then be easy.

1. Shift your weight from one hip to the other. Stand with your feet slightly apart and your hands on your hips. Push your right hand up by lifting your right hip. Your heel will lift off the ground. Feel how the other hip and foot are now weight-loaded. Repeat the exercise on your other side, loading your right foot by lifting your left hip. Practise until it's easy.

2. The action of the unilateral seat aid used to improve the walk and for the canter depart places more pressure on your active seat bone. Stand on your right leg and tighten your right buttock to straighten your hip while keeping your left leg slightly flexed. Relax, then repeat the contraction/relaxation a few times. Repeat the exercise on your left side. Once it is easy, alternate tightening one buttock and then the other. Then try it seated. It is more difficult seated because the contraction of this group of muscles (the hamstrings) straightens the hips.

Mounted body awareness exercises

1. Bend over sideways, from your waist, to the right. On which seat bone does your weight move? It moves to the opposite, left, seat bone. This illustrates the body's rearrangement around its centre of gravity (see also page 42 in Chapter 3).

2. Circle your pelvis around the saddle and feel each part press into the saddle and the opposite part lift, as your hips circle. Repeat to the other side and compare which circle direction is easier. Practise until they are equally easy. This proves that you can place your weight anywhere on the saddle. Take note of the effect of each hip position on your legs.

THE WEIGHT AIDS IN ACTION

The following are descriptions of the aids and their actions, together with further exercises to help you establish the feel and how to use them effectively.

Weight and seat aids for forward and backward movements

1. Tilt your pelvis forwards and back. Try to feel which muscles contract. You will use your abdominal muscles to tilt your pelvis backwards and roll your seat forwards. This is a forward-pushing action and weight aid used when changing from rein-back to forward movement. However, it initiates the flexor pattern and can lead to unsightly rounding of the back and shoulders. Lighten your seat by tilting your pelvis forwards. Your lower back muscles contract, which hollows your back and points your seat up. It rolls your seat backwards. This is the rein-back signal.

The forwards and backwards tilting of the pelvic bone in the saddle, and the muscles responsible for this action:
a) neutral position with the core muscles in balance; b) forward tilt with the back muscle contraction hollowing the back; c) backward tilt with the abdominal muscle contraction rounding the back.

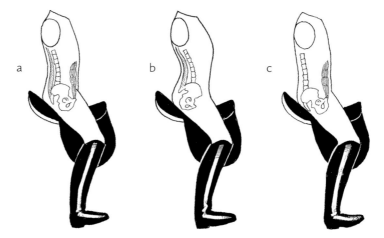

2. Contract the top of your hamstring muscles for forward movement. This puts weight into the seat, moving your seat bones from back to front. Place your hands underneath and slightly in front of your seat bones. Push your hands forwards with your seat muscles and feel how contracting your hamstring muscles can assist in producing impulsion, engagement and extended movements. When you tighten your hamstrings, your abdominals automatically join in.

3. You can also imagine that you are pushing both seat bones closer to your pubic bone. This, together with slight backward-tilting of the pelvis, pushes the horse forwards and promotes engagement of the hindquarters. It is often referred to as the 'driving seat aid'.

4. Close your knees, close your fists and, in split seconds, employ calf pressure, tighten your hamstring muscles a little and stretch up for an energising half-halt in the trot.

5. Place one hand under your one seat bone. Alternate contracting the top of one hamstring with the other. Push your hand forwards using only one side's seat muscles. Repeat with the hamstrings of your other leg to learn how to use them separately to improve the walk strides.

6. Tighten your abdominal and hamstring muscles. This action tilts the pelvis backwards, pushes the hips forwards and rounds the lower back. Müseler called it 'bracing the back'.[1] This action can be used for forward movement, but is an unsightly aid. (The concept of 'bracing the back' is explored in more detail in the next section.)

7. The canter seat aid. Pinch your buttock cheeks together (contraction of the gluteal muscles), then release them. This is used at each stride of the canter to 'lift' and collect the horse, 'picking up' each stride. Together with the half-halt, stretching up with your upper body, and upward squeezes of the lower legs, it collects the canter and engages the hindquarters.

8. Deepen your seat.

    a. 'Open' your seat by 'smiling' with your seat 'cheeks'. This deepens the seat and rotates your hips inwards. The latter points your toes forwards. This 'smiling' helps your seat relax to move with the horse in sitting trot.

    b. Place your hands under your seat bones. Push down on your hands without leaning back. Feel the slight increase of pressure deepening your seat.

    c. Feel your seat deepen and the increase of pressure on your seat bones when you push out your belly button without hollowing your back.

    d. You can also feel this by breathing out and simultaneously pushing out your stomach.

Place your finger against your belly button and push it away without hollowing your back.

9. 'Cease your seat movements' for downward transitions. Stretch up to lighten your seat and brace your waist muscles. Imagine pushing against a tight tube around your waist. This action tightens the lower back and abdominal muscles in co-contraction. It ceases all movement in your lower back.

10. Cease your hip movements for collection and half-halt to energise the trot.

11. The seat aid to medium trot. This is variable depending on the requirement at the time.

    a. Stretch your upper body, allowing the feeling of a very slight gap between the saddle and your seat. (It is not really a gap.) Contract the top of your hamstring muscles. This is one of the most satisfying aids, to which horses respond readily once they are ready to lengthen the trot. Allow bigger hip/waist movements together with the horse's lengthening. Allow your hips to swing left and right, forward and back, together with the larger strides.

    b. The 'driving' seat aid is sometimes used for lengthened strides.

    c. Slowly add calf pressure once the horse responds to seat pressure. Sudden leg pressure will unbalance the horse, causing tightening of his topline with the consequent running, falling on the forehand or breaking into canter.

These aids are given when necessary, but are not maintained, or the horse will stop responding.

Bracing the back

This phrase is often used, but seems to mean different things to different riders. It took me twenty years to understand the concept. What we do know is that bracing the back means contracting certain muscle groups. The word 'brace' means to 'fasten tightly', 'to give firmness'[2] or support. The following are all interpretations of bracing the back.

1. Müseler compared this action to pushing a swing forward with your seat.[3] The swinger leans back to push the swing forwards. This action tightens the abdominal muscles to tilt the pelvis back, but the rounded back is unsightly.

2. 'Bloat' your waist and back by pushing out below your belly button, by pushing an imaginary tube around your trunk, or place your hand on your abdomen and push it away without hollowing your back, as explained above. Feel your waist harden. This is centring. It deepens the seat and prevents the horse from pulling you out of the saddle. It is the result of the contraction of the diaphragm which pushes the viscera against the abdominal wall. This creates pressure in the abdomen, tightening and hardening the wall.

3. Lean backwards. The hip extensors tighten imperceptibly and the abdominal muscles stabilise the torso against gravity. This action, often seen in dressage, pushes the horse forwards, but places the rider behind the movement.

4. Through trial and error I found that bracing the back tightens and straightens the entire spine deep into the saddle. The correct action opens and lifts the rib-cage, straightens and depresses the shoulder blades (maintaining the correct

rotation) and pushes the spine straight down into a deeper seat. It straightens the neck and pushes the chin in slightly. This is core muscle contraction which produces the perfect sitting trot and canter position. It is an important aid because it braces the entire spine. All this is achieved by simply tightening the muscles in between the lower centre borders of the shoulder blades (scapulae). They rotate, bringing the 'wingtips' closer together. You may need someone to trace the area between your shoulder blades to give you the feeling of which muscles to contract. Relax after each contraction for your horse to feel the pressure change.

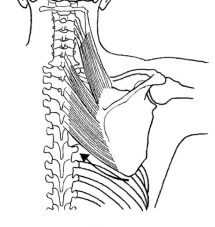

The rhomboid action.

This bracing also teaches the horse to stop from back muscle contraction, thus improving your halts and half-halts. Some horses react immediately to the first bracing in the downward transition; most need only three repetitions. Eventually you can use only this action for downward transitions. Once you have practised this bracing of the back, you will start to use it instinctively and appropriately for the movement concerned.

Learning how to brace the back in this manner is usually a 'light-bulb' moment. Together with pushing out the abdomen (bearing out) it strengthens the seat and prevents the horse from pulling the rider out of the saddle.

Weight and seat aids for bend, lateral movements and canter depart

1. For the canter depart seat aid, pinch the hamstrings of your inside seat inwards. Used together with the inside lower leg, it constitutes the canter aid. However, horses have to be positioned correctly to take the correct canter lead.

2. Place your hand under your one buttock. Using your seat muscles (hamstrings and adductors), push your hand sideways and forwards and feel the contraction of your hamstrings and adductors. This, together with your leg, knee and side muscles, is the weight aid for all lateral movements and pirouettes. This action also prevents the horse from 'falling in'. As you feel the horse begin to worm out from underneath your inside seat bone, push your seat bone down and inwards on the same side to push him back.

3. 'Bloat' the whole side of your body and push it over together with your seat and leg. The leg adductors and the internal abdominal oblique muscles on the same side are in the same functional sling. Adding the contraction of these abdominal muscles increases your effectiveness and helps to maintain your upright position in all lateral movements.

left The hamstring and adductor muscles at the back of the thigh.

right The internal and external abdominal oblique muscles.

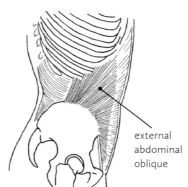

external abdominal oblique

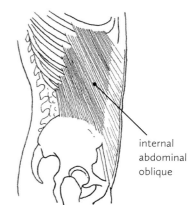

internal abdominal oblique

4. Step into the stirrup and weight it by lifting your opposite hip. Your pelvis tilts laterally (the external and internal abdominal oblique and quadratus lumborum muscles contract). Your waist bends on the lifted side while it stretches on the weighted side. Repeat the exercise on the other side. This action lowers your leg and helps to curl it around the horse when pushing him laterally.

Weight 'aids' to avoid when turning

The following instructions are often used to teach riders to turn. However, they have the opposite effect of that intended.

- Sit slightly to the inside, or sit more firmly on the inner seat bone.

- Shift your weight in the direction of the turn.

- Step into the inside stirrup. The stirrup will pull the horse so that his shoulder 'falls in'.

Horse's reactions to these 'aids' are variable, depending on their training. These instructions and movements appear to make little or no difference to completely untrained horses, or to horses trained to bend correctly. As mentioned earlier, riders' movements are meaningless until horses understand them and recognise their intentions. Seat aids, as with leg aids, are learnt behaviour. When turning, your inside leg should push the horse's ribcage out to move the horse's centre of gravity to balance him around the turn/circle. His head and neck then bend to the inside, in counterbalance. Your weight automatically moves to your outside seat bone.

Chapter 9

LEG USE

THE RIDER'S LEG USE forms the foundation of rider-horse communication. Our legs are our strongest tools of communication. However, riders generally are not leg-aware and tend to correct mistakes too often with their hands rather than with their legs. This is because our hands are more coordinated and are used for most complicated tasks. In normal activities, we use our legs mainly for ambulation and not for complex coordinated skills. In riding we have to develop them, in strength and coordination, to become skilled instruments of communication. The more effective the leg use becomes, the less hand use is necessary in horse-rider communication. Used correctly and with a little direction from the hands, the legs move the horse's body in five directions – forwards, backwards, to the left, to the right and even upwards into more elevation. They shift the horse's ribcage and move his hindquarters; they assist in moving the horse's shoulders. Together with the hands, they produce engagement and collection. On their own, however, they have little effect on rounding the horse's head and neck.

A large percentage of riders do not use their legs for anything other than kicking the horse forwards. Most riders do not know how to dissociate the movement between their legs. The ultimate goal is to be able to use each leg either individually or together with the other one in different positions on the horse. They should be used with different intensities of pressure and with correct timing. The rider's hands should not lock in associated movements with difficult leg movements. Examples of associated movements connected to leg use are:

- Leaning over in lateral movements.

- The inside hand pulling on the rein when the inside leg is pushing the horse laterally.

- The inside leg stops pushing when the inside hand releases.

- The outside leg pushes when only the inside leg should push in shoulder-in and leg-yielding.

- The inside leg pushes too much when the outside leg is used in half-pass and walk pirouette.

STRONG LEGS, LIGHT AIDS

Although leg aids become light once the horse understands the aid, riders need strong legs. The stronger the legs, the easier it is to apply light pressure followed by strong pressure. Strong legs are more convincing. The stronger and more effective the leg action is in bending the horse and moving the horse sideways, the less inside rein the rider will need. This holds true especially on the rider's weak side.

That said, the desirable end product of pressure-release training is a horse who reacts to light leg aids. Constant pressure, whether in the form of continuous kicking, ever-stronger kicking or continuous spur-jabbing, desensitises horses into habituation. Riders have to decide which quality of light pressure suits them best. This pressure is applied and if the horse does not react, it is followed instantly with strong enough pressure to achieve the required result of a forward or a sideways step. All pressure is then released until the horse shows the first sign of slowing down or insensitivity. The process is then repeated until the horse maintains the same sensitivity to each aid.

When to use pressure with both legs together

You should apply bilateral calf pressure for forward movement during all trot work. During the canter, pressure is applied with both calves to 'lift' the canter at each stride. However, sometimes an inside calf tap prevents the horse from breaking from canter into trot. Bilateral thigh/knee pressure is applied for all downward transitions and half-halts. Riders should ensure that this is not accompanied by simultaneous calf pressure, which would give opposing messages.

Leg pressure in the half-halt

There are two forms of half-halt.

1. **The balancing half-halt.** This form of the half-halt is used during the training of young horses. It prepares the young horse for turns, circles, changing direction and going into corners. It is generally used when a young horse's trot changes to a faster rhythm or speed. Start by feathering/vibrating the reins to explain that the horse should not lift and use his neck for balance. Follow with bilateral knee pressure and then two-handed elbow tightening. This is followed by the complete release of both knees and arms as the horse slows down. Light feathering of the reins may continue throughout the half-halt to prevent the head and neck from lifting. The horse will hesitate and slow his rhythm. He will soon respond appropriately to the leg pressures without the need of hand pressure.

2. **The classical half-halt.** This is the energy-producing half-halt. It balances the horse, collects him and promotes elevating energy and cadence. Activate the horse's hind legs with calf pressure. Follow this, in split-second timing, with squeezing both knees/thighs and then tightening both hands/arms to give a slowing down aid. An infinitesimal time space separates the energising calf pressure and the slowing down knee and hand pressure. Repeat these actions to produce more engagement of the hindquarters, especially in the canter and passage.

Leg pressure in the halt

Knee/thigh pressure alone is used initially when teaching young horses and novice riders to halt. Riders first have to learn to dissociate the knee and the calf pressure, while the young horse should not be given opposing aids. Once the horse understands this halt aid, calf pressure is added, almost simultaneously but split seconds after the knee pressure, to square up the forelegs. Apply knee pressure and add squeezing calf pressure, in a crescendo manner, as the horse takes the last walk step. 'Catch' the squaring-up step with the rein on the same side. Watch his shoulders to correlate the squaring up. You can dictate the size of the last step with the degree of rein tension. Use tighter tension for a short step and looser tension for a longer step.

Square up the hind legs by adding a little foot-tapping split seconds after, but without removing, the calf pressure. It sounds strange, but it works. The sequence is thus: finger-feathering to maintain the yielding – knee pressure for halting – locking elbows if the knee pressure alone is not effective – calf pressure to square up the forelimbs – rein pressure to dictate the size of the squaring-up step and finally foot-tapping/jiggling to square up the hind legs.

Unilateral leg aids

Unilateral leg pressure is used for bend, the canter, the rein-back and to ask the horse to move sideways. It is also used, in lateral movements, to ask for activity when the other leg asks for lateral steps. Unilateral leg aids are often accompanied by unilateral seat aids. The position of the leg in relation to the horse's centre of gravity is important. In front of the centre of gravity it moves the shoulders sideways. In the area of the centre of gravity it moves the horse's ribcage. Behind the centre of gravity it moves the hindquarters sideways.

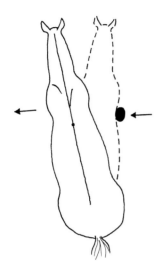

Leg pressure in front of the withers moves the horse's shoulders.

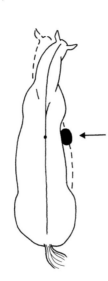

Leg pressure on the ribcage shifts the horse's ribcage.

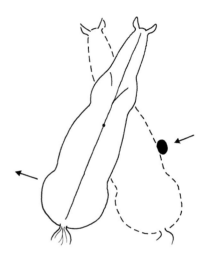

Leg pressure further back, moves the horse's hindquarters.

Unilateral leg pressure for bend

The inside leg is used, in its natural position, to push the ribcage to the outside and produce an inside bend. The horse will place more weight on his outside legs and counterbalance by turning his head to the same side as the pushing leg. Push against the horse's ribcage with the calf of your inside leg only. Vibrate the inside rein together with the leg pressure, to ask the horse to bend from his head and neck through his body. These aids are used for bending, turns, circles, spirals and serpentines.

For inside bend, the outside leg is not initially needed. As mentioned earlier, adding the outside leg before a rider is well coordinated causes opposing messages. The outside leg will automatically fall against the horse's side once it has become passive. Once riders have learnt the walk pirouette, this leg will automatically become active positioned slightly back in the above movements, especially during small circles and turns.

Unilateral leg pressure in lateral movements

The inside leg is used in its neutral position, hanging below the hip, to push the horse's ribcage for bend and shoulder-in. However, in the initial stages of learning the shoulder-in, riders are more effective when using the leg further back. Young horses also learn the concept with greater ease when the rider's leg pressure is further back.

In the turn on the forehand, leg-yield and half-pass, the leg pressure should move the horse's hindquarters. Therefore, it should be well behind the horse's centre of gravity.

It is best to use the whole leg together with the lateral-pushing seat. You should also tighten your side muscles and move them over. Lateral work encompasses a coordinated system incorporating almost the whole one side of your body.

Leg-yielding.

Unilateral leg pressure in front of the centre of gravity

Leg pressure in front of the centre of gravity moves the horse's shoulders. Young horses often 'fall in' on circles (especially to one side). The fastest method of stopping this is to move your inside leg forwards, although this seems a method rarely taught. Apply light pressure in this position, followed up instantly with a whip tap. The horse will immediately move his shoulders sideways. Three repetitions of this pressure, followed by a whip tap, will be enough to teach the horse to move his shoulders out with light leg pressure only. Use this aid whenever the horse 'falls in or out' or moves his shoulders over too fast in lateral work.

Use leg pressure in a slightly forward position to move the horse's shoulders out.

Alternate single leg pressure for rein-back

Horses appear to understand the rein-back better when alternating unilateral leg pressure is used. Halt your horse using a series of half-halts into the halt. This ensures that he does not move weight onto his shoulders. Lighten your seat by tilting your pelvis forwards to give the horse the signal that the rein-back is imminent. Lock your elbows to block forward movement. Feather with your fingers to explain to the horse that he is not to lift his head and hollow in the rein-back. Use alternate calf pressure to ask the horse to step back in diagonal pairs.

A good rein-back is a rare occurrence in the lower levels of dressage. The classical rein-back, using bilateral calf pressure together with blocking rein pressure, is another example of opposing messages. Shortly after halting, horses move 60 per cent of their weight onto their forelimbs. The horse's first reaction, when both the rider's legs are used together, is to lean forwards in preparation for a forward step, thus more weight moves onto his forehand, making it difficult to take a backward step. He may drag his feet, shuffle back or take hesitant steps. Alternate calf pressure for the rein-back distinguishes it from the bilateral calf pressure used for forward movement. The horse therefore does not lean forwards. This ensures large steps.

Releasing the knee grip

To release knee pressure, relax your adductor muscles. Riders who find it difficult to break the knee-gripping habit should push down on their heels. This extensor pattern, activated by the downward-pushing heels, leads to the automatic external rotation of the knees. It turns the knees slightly away from the saddle. This is especially important during jumping: it prevents the lower legs from swinging back and the upper body from lurching forwards beyond its centre of gravity. The rider is thus less likely to lose balance or fall.

THE LEGS AS WEIGHT AIDS

'Stepping into', or putting more weight on the inside foot, has no effect when riding bareback. Stepping into a stirrup however, is a leg aid which is, in reality, a weight aid through its effect on the saddle. The weight in the stirrup 'pulls' the saddle to the side. The horse feels this pull and follows the movement as he would follow the rein aid. The stirrup leather thus functions as a 'leg rein' pulling the horse to the side. We have been describing this riding tool inadvertently for many years as 'stepping into the inside stirrup'. We can use this tool far more effectively if we know how its biomechanics work.

Stepping into the stirrup

Stepping into the *outside* stirrup is used to prevent the horse from 'falling in' on turns and circles. It is used together with the inside leg and seat, which push the horse's ribcage and weight to the outside. Rein-feathering for inside neck bend completes the explanation.

When the horse develops a habit of 'falling in', step into the outside stirrup. Push your heel down and your lower leg out a little and straighten your knee slightly. Push his ribcage over simultaneously with your inside leg. The horse will follow the pulling pressure of your outside leg in the stirrup and move his shoulder out and, as a consequence, bend his neck in. After a few repetitions, the stepping out becomes an invisible slight weighting of the outside stirrup. When you use this as an adjunct to inside leg pressure, the horse will soon move out on inside leg pressure alone.

Stepping into the *inside* stirrup has the opposite effect and is not desirable; your inside stirrup leather pulls the horse, encouraging him to 'fall in'. He moves his head to the outside, with consequent loss of bend.

Stepping out into the outside stirrup, while pushing the ribcage with the inside leg, will move the horse's shoulder out.

Chapter 10

‖‖

HAND USE – PRINCIPLES

OUR HANDS ARE OUR most delicate tools of feel. The blind use them to read language; mothers use them to caress their babies; lovers use them to pass on the message of love. They are used to produce the most beautiful music as they stroke piano keys. Thus, for superior and sophisticated communication with the horse, we need to develop superior feel and coordination in our fingers.

The great classical masters recommended movement of the hands in pressure-release actions. However, the delicate and detailed communication between the riders' hands and the horse' mouth has been sadly neglected for many years. I have heard and read phrases such as 'the hands are the least important aspect of riding' and 'the hands are only accessories.' If this is a common philosophy in teaching riding, there is not too much hope for the poor horse's mouth or for his under-standing of the rider.

The hands are, in fact, the most important aspect of riding because they can make or break a horse's mouth. During my many years of teaching I have found that the majority of riders hang onto their horse's mouths. This seems to be the biggest single stumbling block in learning the art of riding. Mouth problems are arguably the most common horse and rider problems encountered. Unless there is underlying pathology, they are all caused by incorrect hand use. The many requests for help in the horsy magazines are evidence to this: 'My horse won't come on the bit'; 'I'm not strong enough to keep him on the bit'; 'My horse is heavy in my hands/ hangs on my hands'; 'My horse is hard in the mouth'; 'My horse pulls/resists'; 'My horse won't slow down'; 'My horse runs away with me'; 'My horse rushes the jumps'; 'I have a big strong horse and therefore he takes a strong contact'. These are but a few of the problems discussed.

> **EVERY RIDER I HAVE TAUGHT** started off with hand/arm problems and therefore also horse problems. When their arms, shoulders and hands became loose, relaxed and free from tension, their horses all managed to work through in a round flexor frame. These riders all needed no more than three lessons to correct their hand/arm use. See upper photos on page 34, and on page 155.

These problems are completely solvable with correct hand use, without resorting to stronger bits. Most of the ancient paintings, sculptures and friezes depicting horses, show their mouths open in pain. The modern method is to camouflage the pained open mouth with tight nosebands. Is it not time that we learnt correct hand use which does not cause pain in horses' mouths?

DESTRUCTIVE PHRASES IN TEACHING

Riders are generally taught how *not* to use their hands and arms instead of how to use them correctly. The functions of the hands and arms are narrowed down to the rhetorical phrases such as, 'hold your hands still'; 'do nothing with your hands'; 'don't move your hands'; 'steady your hands'; 'keep your hands quiet'; 'carry your hands' and 'don't fiddle'. The exact position of 10cm (4in) apart, 10cm (4in) above the withers and 10cm (4in) in front of the body is often plotted and in fact, called 'the four-inch rule'. This rule has a particularly bad effect on the horse's mouth because riders' arms become rigid and lose all elastic contact as they focus on maintaining this exact position. All these instructions are destructive because novice riders do not understand them and they have the opposite effect from that intended on both horse and rider.

The fixation on 'keeping the hands still' has, arguably, done more damage to the horse's and rider's ability to perform than any other single factor in modern riding technique. It has created generations of riders with rigid, incorrectly used elbows, shoulders and hands. It has caused many, if not most, of the mouth and contact problems encountered in riding. This is one of the reasons why Warmblood horses are so popular – many tolerate riders hanging on their mouths.

In addition to being technically inappropriate, this 'nothingness' with the hands has another negative aspect: we cannot learn by doing nothing; we achieve nothing and the horse is kept in the dark. Here are some reasons why such teaching is counterproductive:

- Attempting to 'keep the hands still', 'steady the hands', 'carry the hands' and even 'do nothing' all need permanent muscle contraction, usually co-contraction of the arm, hand and shoulder muscles, which results in stiffness. The biceps muscles contract, tighten the elbows and move the hands back, thus pulling on the horse's mouth. The hands become hard and 'dead'. These rigid arms exert a continuous pressure (pulling/hanging) on the horse's mouth. They cannot yield and all elastic contact is lost.

- During rising trot these 'still' hands actually move up and down from the withers, causing inconsistent pressure on the bars and tongue of the horse's mouth, at every stride. The horse cannot maintain a steady flexor frame. The meaningless changes of pressure of the bit in his mouth are uncomfortable, even painful.

A VISUAL CLUE OF ELBOW rigidity is when the hands stay equidistant from the rider's body, but they move up and down from the withers in rising trot. The only way the hands can maintain the same relative distance from the horse's withers during posting is if the elbows are relaxed, opening and closing at every stride.

Fingers resting on the withers prevents them from lifting during the rising phase of the trot. It results in a soft, elastic contact with opening and closing elbows.

- The rigidity and 'dead' pressure of riders' arms and hands, which these phrases have created, kill the sensitivity in the horse's mouth. They have created too many horses with hard, 'deadened', resisting mouths (horses resist because riders pull/

resist). Constant pressure on the bars of the horse's mouth, when keeping the hands still, can cause permanent damage to the delicate nerve endings. Compare this with sitting on a chair which causes pressure under your thighs. The painful pins and needles feeling in your feet is the result of constant pressure on the nerves. After ten minutes you have to move your legs to relieve the pain in your feet, or your feet become numb. After a while you will lose sensation in your feet. If you continue to sit without relieving the pressure (but you won't!), your nerves become damaged and your legs become paralysed. This is what happens in a horse's mouth. Horses first attempt to relieve the pressure by overflexing. If the pressure continues, they lift their heads. These actions *should* tell the riders that the pressure is incorrect, but when the pressure continues the horses habituate to it and lose sensitivity in the same way that they habituate to constant leg-clamping on their sides. Eventually, they lose all sensation. Contact and rein aids thus become ever stronger.

- Rigidity prevents feel awareness, which is only possible through a soft rein contact. It kills hand sensitivity, and together with the rigidity, prevents intricate communication with the horse. When riders do nothing with their hands there is no meaningful pressure-release communication. The horse has to second-guess the rider and cannot understand or learn. Half-halts, the round flexor frame and bend are not possible when doing nothing. By 'doing nothing' with their hands, riders cannot learn the correct feel and timing of the pressure-reaction-release.

- All the phrases mentioned block forward movement because hand and arm rigidity cause slowing down bit pressure.

- This method of developing contact by doing nothing or keeping the hands still usually takes unnecessarily long. The 'on the bit' frame remains a mystery to the rider and becomes an obsession.

- The instruction, 'Keep your elbows by your sides' is another destructive phrase which should be deleted from riding tuition. Riders interpret this instruction in two ways.
  a. They inevitably take their arms back and lock their elbows and shoulders, causing stiff elbow and shoulder joints.
  b. When riders interpret it as meaning to avoid the elbows protruding laterally, they clamp their elbows rigidly against their sides.

Elastic contact is impossible when riders' elbows are set against their sides. Hard-and-fast rules cannot apply to how close the elbows should be to the rider's sides in the sagittal plane (from front to back). The length of the rider's arms dictates the closeness to their sides (see photos opposite).

The common rigid arm position of the short-armed rider in her first lesson. She is also rising too upright and thus behind the movement, causing defensive mouth behaviour in the horse. This rider's tight arms and the horse's anxiety were transformed into harmony in three lessons.

In lesson three the rider's arms are relaxed, her position stayed with the movement and the horse became relaxed, with flowing movement. Even the rider's arms do not appear short when used correctly.

Turned-in hands cause the elbows to protrude. Correct this by rotating your forearms outwards. Simply turn your thumbs into the uppermost position, with your knuckles facing each other. This points each thumb towards the horse's opposite ear, which softens your wrists. It does not produce tension, but gives the hands, wrists and forearms more freedom to move and communicate through the reins.

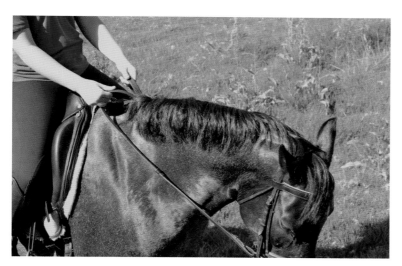

Thumbs uppermost, facing horse's opposite ears.

- The term 'take up the contact' is another destructive phrase. It seems to be interpreted as taking a hold on the reins and is often used each time the horse is about to trot. Pressure on the bit increases with the first step into trot. The brakes are thus used both before and together with the accelerator.

Very sincere attempts and good intentions to protect horses' mouths have back-fired through using these phrases to instruct. There seems to be a great fear that, by moving their hands, riders will learn to use them badly and hurt the horse's mouth. In fact, only by learning to use the hands correctly, with well-developed fine motor coordination, can the bad-hand syndrome be overcome. Nuno Oliveira said: 'Students of dressage must be taught to use their hands and legs in a proper fashion.'[1] Gustav Steinbrecht said, 'The trainer must know how to use these different hand aids, often in rapid succession.'[2] Experienced riders and those with exceptional feel, timing and coordination, riding horses with unspoiled mouths, *appear* to 'do nothing'. The rest first have to learn to use their hands correctly.

SOME TIME AGO, Judith had great difficulty maintaining a steady 'on the bit' contact even though her horse had a particularly soft and easy mouth. In desperation I decided to demonstrate, together with a running commentary. To my surprise, by verbalising my feel, I realised that I was automatically making constant minute finger adjustments to every small action of the horse's mouth, head and neck. My fingers could feel what the horse was about to do with his head and neck. They automatically prevented him from going above or behind the bit, or hollowing his neck. My fingers vibrated like butterfly wings explaining to the horse not to lift his head. These movements were invisible to the observer. I realised then that riders with automatic feel are often not aware of the small, instantaneous reactions and adjustments of each body part, when exerting perfect control over their horses. Before I became aware of these tiny finger adjustments, I could not teach them.

Changing the terminology

The horse's mouth is 'sacred ground'. It should never be abused, punished, used for balance or held with constant pressure. The *intended* meaning of all the above instructions, regarding 'doing nothing' with the hands, is that the arms and shoulders should relax, move with the horse's mouth and yield when the horse yields. They should exert no pressure on the bars and tongue of the horse's mouth unless requesting an action. This gives *an appearance* of being still because their movement is relative to the movement of the horse's head and neck. Gustav Steinbrecht said: 'The rider must, to the contrary, freely balance his arms by keeping their joints relaxed so as to absorb any shocks in the arms themselves and thus maintain the hands steady.'[3]

On teaching michael to relax his elbows in our first lesson, his reaction was, 'OK, I'll relax them, but don't expect me to hold my hands still then.' He had been doing what all riders do when trying to keep their hands still – tightening them. It had exactly the opposite effect. By the end of the first lesson the horse accepted the bit for the first time and adopted the correct round flexor frame. All Michael had done was to relax his arms.

The destructive phrases and instructions have to be replaced with more appropriate teaching terminology. This is important for the physical and mental well-being of the horse. The following phrases are most effective for correcting hand use. They all contribute to the development of good hands. These are: 'relax your arms'; 'relax/release your elbows'; 'relax your upper arms/shoulders'; 'allow your arms to move forward with the horse's mouth/head; 'soften your elbows'; 'soften your arms'; 'breathe through your arms'; 'drop your hands on the withers/saddle'; and 'take and *give*'. The location of the tightness should be assessed and addressed.

When i started riding, I was taught to ride with floppy reins and to give continuously. I learnt to do everything with my legs and seat. Consequently my ex-racehorse became very obedient to my legs and very light in hand. However, I could not manage the round flexor 'on the bit' frame. At our first show, he came 'on the bit' all by himself. At the time I had no idea how this had happened. Today I realise that the horse must have become more animated and I, a little tense. This probably led to a slightly stronger, yet elastic contact. The horse yielded to the pressure because he had never learnt defensive mouth behaviour. He gave me the perfect feel of contact.

Over the course of time, I became a guinea pig to all the fads that each new teacher was trying out. Some of these are as follows:

- Take and give with the inside hand only – this was incorrectly called a 'half-halt'.

- Take and give with alternate hands. This became sawing.

- Strong contact on the outside rein. This turned the horse's head out and is the cause of many horses today not bending correctly through corners, circles and turns.

- Holding the contact in both reins while 'pushing the horse into the contact'. This is still leading to hard/dead mouths.

Through experimentation, I finally found an eclectic method of keeping my horse steady and light on the bit. What I found was a myriad of hand and finger movements, which were all meaningful to the horse. I squeezed whichever rein at whatever strength and frequency was necessary to elicit the correct reaction from the horse. I yielded automatically when the horse yielded. We had a constant conversation through light finger and hand actions.

CONTACT

No treatise on hand use can be complete without a discussion regarding contact. Contact has two functions:

1. Communication through the horse's mouth.

2. Producing the 'on the bit' frame. This is lightness and balanced self-carriage, in the correct yielding, round flexor frame. The best definition I have been able to find for 'on the bit' and contact, is from the great French masters who named it the *ramener*:

> The *ramener* is less a direction or position of the head: rather it is a general state of the submission and pliancy of the horse's joints and muscles. It lies, first of all, in the submission of the jaw which is the first joint that receives the effect of the hand. If, on the other hand, the jaw resists or refuses to be mobilised, there is no lightness.[4]

(Although it is not just the jaw that has to relax, but also the poll and neck muscles.) The frame is thus 'on the bit', but it is the consequences that are important:

- It produces superb lightness.

- It improves regularity, rhythm, balance, suppleness and 'throughness'. The movement thus flows and bending is easy.

- It inhibits his neck balance reactions: the horse has to use his hips and hind legs for balance.

- This flexor frame facilitates bringing the horse's hindquarters underneath his body for engagement and controls the quality of the engagement. (The hollow frame 'disengages' the hindquarters.)

- The round flexor frame strengthens the horse's back for riding.

- Collection and extensions are dependent on this flexor carriage.

- The success of all advanced movements is dependent on the horse maintaining the correct, soft flexor frame although, in their forms as working exercises, they also help in the development of this frame.

Sadly, the interpretation of the word contact has, in many cases, been corrupted. Phrases such as, 'take up the contact', 'ride the horse into contact' and 'support or hold the horse' (into a fence) have produced an impression that contact should be firm. The amount of contact taught is often too strong, causing undue pressure on horses' mouths. Believing that a horse should habitually be held into a fence is as presumptuous as trying to lift the horse over the fence. This practice often results in hands which do not move forwards with the horse's mouth. It is unlikely to improve his attitude or technique.

Contact means touch. It can be interpreted as the feeling of two fingers touching or the feeling of the pull in a tug-of-war game, and everything in between, depending on the interpretation of the rider and trainer.

The horse's mouth and the bit

There is no real space in the horse's mouth for the bit. There is only potential space. The horse's tongue fills the entire cavity, lying against the palate, against the mouth floor, over the bars and against the cheeks. All bits make their own space by pressing down the tongue and pressing against the palate. When there is no tension on the reins, the bit does not touch the bars. When riding on contact, pressure is placed continuously on the bars while depressing the tongue. Tongue pressure causes the automatic tongue-thrust reflex. The horse pushes his tongue against the foreign object in an attempt to remove it. It is a major cause of the tongue slipping over the bit and the protruding tongue. If the horse's tongue is particularly large, it can protrude constantly. Horses have no gag reflex, which means that the tongue-thrust reflex is particularly strong in these animals. The double-jointed bit with a central lozenge appears to be a major cause of the tongue-thrust reflex. The curb bit causes enormous pressure on the palate, the tongue, the jaw

Note Fritz
Stahlecker has
designed a kinder
curb bit for the
double bridle. It
conforms to all FEI
requirements and
causes less pressure
on the bars.

and especially the bars of the horse's mouth.* As the reins pull the shanks down, the sides of the mouthpiece, exactly where it curves, press harder onto the bars. The tongue is squashed between the bars and the hard metal while the curb hits the palate.

The wrong supposition!

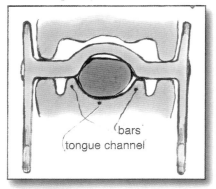

The reality!

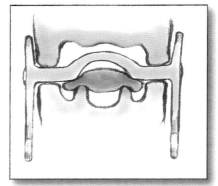

The pressure caused by the curb bit on the bars and tongue. Illustration by Fritz Stahlecker, reproduced with permission.

Light contact

Damage to the nerves of the bars, with the consequent loss of sensation and the tongue-thrust reflex, are the main reasons why light contact is non-negotiable. Self-carriage is light contact with the hindquarters carrying the weight. Riders have to aim for the lightest contact that will pass the message on to the horse, whether the horse is in the round flexor, 'on the bit' frame, or in the natural frame. Contact in dressage, means the soft feel when the horse is in the form of '*ramener*' as defined by L'Hotte, Oliveira and others. Anything harder is caused by incorrect riding because contact becomes stronger when the horse loses self-carriage, is balancing on his forehand and thus pulls down, or when he opens the angle of the poll and moves into a hollow frame, using his extensor (topline) muscles against the pull of the bit. He may only appear to be 'on the bit'.

Top riders through the ages from Xenophon, through De la Guérinière, Baucher and Steinbrecht to the present, are all in agreement about lightness. However, lightness means different qualities to different riders. In the seventeenth century, the Duke of Newcastle wrote: 'He must be light in hand, because no horse can be rightly upon his haunches without being so ... no horse therefore is well dressed that is not light in hand ... he [the rider] ought to feel very little of the bridle.'[5] General L'Hotte had this to say about the rider's hands: 'True lightness consists in having the horse light on the legs as well as [light] on the hand ... the hand not oppos-

The strong contact of tight extensor muscles while appearing to be in a round frame.

ing the forward movement in any way' and, 'teach your horse to go with a light hand on the bit.[6] Nuno Oliveira said, 'A horse may be considered attentive and obedient when he stays well balanced and is light on the rider's hand'[7] and Michel Henriquet, 'The reins must be adjusted to a semi-tension, that is, the weight of the leather'.[8] More modern riders such as Tineke Bartels say, 'Training is ultimately aimed at making the forehand light and manoeuvrable';[9] Ulla Saltzgeber, 'Create a light connection with the horse's mouth … every horse needs to learn to move on his own without support from the rider.[10] Johann Hinnemann recommends that 'The first exercises must aim to make the horse soft in the bridle.'[11]

When the rein contact is loose and floppy, the horse is in self-carriage, but he cannot feel fine finger communications. Without a straight rein contact the horse will not initially learn to yield into the round flexor frame. However, once he has yielded into this frame, the reins can be yielded for a few strides without him losing this 'on the bit' frame. This is de la Guérinière's *descente de main* which is now tested in dressage competitions. It shows that the horse is in self-carriage and not constrained in position. See photos overleaf.

Contact does not mean support as a beam supports a house. When a body is supported, its balance is compromised, not improved. Just as it is for riders, the horse's body has to be set up to balance itself in the different movements we ask of him. If we hold onto the reins and he does not support himself in light self-carriage, he cannot use his balancing tools to maintain balance effectively. Would it not be easier for a horse to do the movements and to jump high, if he were in light contact, balancing himself?

Stronger contact prevents the horse from feeling light finger communications on his bars and lips. For the horse's well-being it is better to err on the side of yielding too much rather than yielding too little.

Straight reins without pulling.

The soft reins of *descente de main* are proof that the horse is in self-carriage.

Contact and the 'on the bit' frame

Contrary to popular belief 'contact' or the round flexor frame is initiated by the horse's head and neck. Horses' flexor muscles work from the head through the abdomen and hips to the hind toes. Hip flexion is essential for engagement; it is this that brings the hindquarters underneath. Contact starts when the reins are picked up. In halt there is no forward movement, yet the horse can maintain the round flexor frame with ease. In fact François Baucher started a horse's training by first 'suppling its neck' for the 'on the bit' mobility. He advocated that the rider first establishes flexion at the poll and yielding of the jaw (the poll and neck) to bit pressure (*ramener*) and then pushes the horse forwards (*rassembler*) in this soft contact. These two together then bring perfect balance. This means that yielding is not initiated by the hindquarters, but instead enhanced by them to produce 'throughness'.

The method of 'riding from the back to the front', 'pushing the hindquarters forwards into contact' increases the painful bit pressure. In the hands of strong and experienced riders it may motivate the horse to yield faster, because these riders can drive the horse through the resistance into a yielding contact. In practice however, this is nothing less than pushing and pulling camouflaged in sugar-coated words because the legs give a forward message while the bit creates pressure. It is not the hindquarters which produce the yielding, but the increased painful bit pressure. This method is often misunderstood and remains a mystery to most novice riders, especially when they have been taught to 'do nothing' with their hands. It is fair to say that probably 90 per cent of horses' problems are connected to incorrect contact and communication from the rider's hands.

The 'on the bit' halt.

As a method of teaching the horse to round correctly into the soft flexor frame it is wrong and it does not work. The proof – most horses have mouth problems. Riders who have not developed sufficient feel create mouth problems. They do not know when to soften the contact or how hard to push to achieve this. Most riders have difficulty finding consistent light contact, and riding 'on the bit' becomes an obsession. By the time these riders want to start riding competition dressage, the tug of war between their hands and their horse's mouths is already in place, together with resistance, pulling and hanging. More mouths are destroyed by this method than through any other riding fault. It leads to ever-tighter nosebands and hyperflexion. The main cause for its failure is that it gives the horse opposing messages, causing anxiety and confusion. So why not simply ask the horse to yield to bit pressure, release as he yields, and then ask him to move forwards in balance together with the round flexor frame?

ABOUT TEN YEARS AGO I was invited to teach this soft method of riding 'hands without legs and legs without hands' in a city in Norway. At the time, their horses apparently did not move forwards and they were hard in the mouth. My initial experience had been mainly with Thoroughbreds and the odd Warmblood horse, all of whom were light in hand and moved forwards with ease. I assumed that their horses were of a different breed. The first course brought one horse after the other who would not move forwards and was either very hard in the mouth or extremely anxious. All the horses had been ridden in the confusing 'forwards into contact' method. Contact was assumed to be firm and holding, while the legs pushed into this. The horses stopped feeling the bit and they stopped feeling the riders' legs. All movement disappeared. A large percentage had developed four-beat canters. It took three to four days to teach the twenty horses to be light and forwards and the canter sequence to be restored. The riders all learnt to be light, through the method of riding 'hands without legs and legs without hands' and all subsequently discarded the old 'pull/push' method.

Horses will only accept a steady and soft/yielding contact in the 'on the bit' frame if they trust the rider's hands. A defensive horse, who fears the rider's hands, will either lift his nose or curl his neck, in an attempt to evade or pull away from painful bit pressure. Incorrect timing of pressure and release, hanging, pulling, rigidity, sawing and jerking all cause distrust in the rider's hands.

When horses maintain self-carriage in the round flexor frame they will stretch their heads and necks slowly forwards and downwards when the reins are released. When riders 'hold' the horse on strong contact he is effectively opposing the contact, using his extensor muscles. This stimulates the stretch reflex as well as causing uncomfortable bit pressure. When the reins are released these horses usually snatch them downwards. The stretch reflex is also stimulated when the round flexor frame is maintained for too long a period.

Elastic contact

Elastic contact is essential to avoid pressure when the horse is in the 'on the bit' flexor frame. It protects the nerve endings in the bars of the horse's mouth and ensures lightness. Elasticity is movement. Only hands, arms and shoulders devoid of tension allow the movement necessary to maintain a consistent elastic connection with the horse's mouth. A block in the system, from the rein to the rider's back, effectively destroys this elasticity. The horse stops moving forwards. Contact should be alive and elastic, never jerky; the latter causes pain. The shoulder joint has to act as the fulcrum to ensure elastic contact and prevent blocking. The elbow joints also open and close as the arms move with the horse's mouth.

ALL TEACHING PRACTICES which block arm movements are counterproductive. They prevent the arms from moving with the horse's head and neck, causing undue pressure on the horse's mouth.

The lungeing exercise in which riders maintain arm position as though holding the reins reinforces elbow and shoulder rigidity and destroys elastic contact.

All the rein exercises mentioned in Chapter 5 improve elastic contact.

above left Securing the upper arms behind the back with an elastic band blocks elasticity, with resultant defensive behaviour from the horse.

above right Holding a stick between the hands causes contact rigidity.

left Lungeing with the hands in 'riding position' causes rigidity.

Elastic contact and slipping reins

Novice riders often ride with open hands, allowing the reins to slip. Unintentional rein slipping releases pressure at the wrong moment, rewarding the horse for non-specific actions. This leads to slower learning for both horse and rider. The reins have to be secured with a strong hold between the baby and ring fingers. This ensures that the hands are not clamped around the reins, causing tightness in the forearms. (See drawing of intrinsic muscles on page 54.)

Prevent the reins from slipping by gripping them between the two fingers.

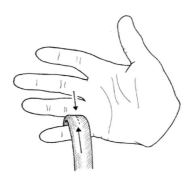 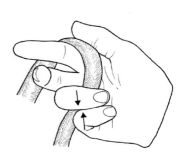

Contact and inside bend

Most dressage movements are performed towards the inside of the arena, and also have an inside bend (*note that 'inside' ultimately refers to the horse, not the arena*), therefore a slight inside bend is needed for the following reasons:

- As preparation before most movements, change of movements and changes of direction.

- For suppling and to ride circles, shoulder-in, half-pass, the canter and pirouettes.

- The inside bend is a major tool for straightening the horse.

- It breaks the extensor pattern.

- A slight inside bend (the 'position') assists and improves balance especially during transitions and circles.

- It develops ambidexterity in the horse when used in both directions.

When the rider's inside leg pushes the horse's ribcage over, the horse's head and neck bend to the inside. When the horse bends his own neck to the inside, the contact on the inside rein becomes lighter. This automatically results in a slightly firmer contact on the outside rein. This is the origin of the phrase, 'ride from your inside leg to your outside rein'.

Use an effective inside leg together with a feathering inside rein for bend instead of taking more contact on the outside rein. A firm outside contact should not be the result of taking a stronger hold on the outside rein; it should be the result of correct bending. The horse does not understand that stronger contact on the outside rein means more bend to the inside; he is not that good at solving riddles. Strong outside contact turns the horse's head out; more inside rein is then needed to bend it in. This defeats the object.

An opening outside rein helps to prevent the shoulders from 'falling in' and so assists maintenance of the opposite bend. Test the correctness of the bend by yielding your inside rein. A loose inside rein indicates that the bend is true. If the horse is bending his own neck he will maintain this bend for a few strides. Beware of the false bend in which it is you pulling the horse to the inside, with a consequent stronger contact, not the horse bending his own neck. If the contact on the outside is lighter than on the inside, the horse is bent incorrectly and the bend is false. Gustav Steinbrecht said, 'The release of the outer side (loose outside rein), is always connected with a false bend.'[12] The horse's balance into the next movement will be compromised and he will 'fall' into the turn or circle. This false bend is a common riding error. Pulling on the inside rein also results in the horse's hindquarters swinging out in the ENR.

An example of the false bend. The horse's head is turned, but he is not yielding to the rein pressure. The inside rein is tight and his inside neck muscles are not visible.

CORRECT USE OF ARMS AND HANDS (FORM FOLLOWS FUNCTION)

Spoilt mouths develop through incorrect use of the rider's hands and arms. We know this because no horse is born with a hard mouth. Every step of training (calmness, rhythm, balance, suppleness, contact, straightness, forwardness and engagement) is adversely affected by 'bad hands'. It is thus vitally important for the protection of the horse's mouth that riders learn to communicate with correct hand and arm use. The hand and arm position must follow function (use of hands and arms), not the other way around, as is generally taught.

'Take and give' and the 'on the bit' frame

Pressure-release, 'take and give', squeeze the reins. These are all the same concept of yielding to pressure. Horses yield to leg pressure by taking forward steps. They yield to single leg pressure by taking lateral steps. They should yield to bit pressure with an immediate reaction of bringing the nose closer to your hands.

The young horse will first yield to bit pressure by dropping his nose. If the training is incorrect and the pressure is not released instantly, he will try other methods of avoiding the pressure. He may lift his nose and try to pull the reins forward. He may shake his head up and down, or open his mouth. He may snatch, pull or hang on the rider's hands in an attempt to pull the reins away. (He may even move his head behind the bit which, from his perspective, is the smart move.) Unfortunately this problem is often addressed by 'taking a stronger contact'. The pulling and hanging will continue because the horse's mouth becomes numb. It is then said that the horse has a hard mouth.

SHORTLY BEFORE WRITING this book, I gave a course in which most of the horses hung on the reins with a low head and neck carriage and pulled the reins forwards and down. It transpired that their regular trainer had been teaching the riders to maintain a consistent contact with their hands by following the horse's head wherever he wanted to carry it. This is, in principle, a good concept, but the trainer had not noticed that the contact was not light and elastic in the first place. The horses were pulling down against the pressure and the riders simply allowed this. This was a clear reward for pulling and the consequence was a continuous pulling/hanging contact. If the contact had originally been light and elastic and the horses wanted to carry their heads low in this light contact, the problem would not have developed.

Together with learning to relax their arms, riders have to learn how to coordinate fine finger movements in this great principle of 'take and give'. The concept of pressure-release, or taking and giving to ask the horse to yield into the round flexor 'on the bit' frame is not, and should never degenerate into, mindless repetitive, rhythmic sponging, nagging, sawing, jiggling or fiddling. It is a meaningful explanation to the horse to focus and not to use his neck for balance, nor to look around in the hollow extensor position. The most important aspect of the pressure-release system of training is that the rider yields instantly or one second after the horse yields or reacts correctly.

All the top trainers, from the earliest, have recommended this method of communicating with the horse. Xenophon said: 'He would receive the bit the more readily if some good should come of it every time he received it ....The moment he acknowledges it [the pressure] and begins to raise [arch] his neck, give him the bit.'[13] De la Guérinière: 'After the half-halt, give with the hand.... For the effect of the gentle hand must always precede and follow the effect of the firm hand.[14] François Baucher: 'Tension is placed on the snaffle reins. As soon as the horse yields, tension on the rein is decreased.[15] Steinbrecht: 'This is accomplished by alternately taking up the reins and yielding so that the horse is unable to find a constant, firm support on the bit but learns to carry itself independently.'[16] James Fillis: 'To obtain this result [yielding of the jaw], combined with lightness, we must continuously practise the great principle of taking and giving; the former to stop resistance, the latter to reward obedience ... educated hands take when he [the horse] takes and gives when he gives.'[17] Alois Podhajsky: 'The aids consist of taking and giving, the latter being of the greater importance ... With young horses the whole arm of the rider must be employed to give the aids.'[18] Anthony Paalman calls this action 'the first rein aid'.[19] Nuno Oliveira explained it as follows: 'When I speak of the hands' action I mean the opening and shutting of the fingers, giving way to the horse when he gives, and resisting firmly when he does not, never taking back on the reins, allowing the hand to resemble a filter.'[20] Molly Sivewright writes: 'Through alternate restraining and giving ...[21] The official German training manual calls it the 'regulating rein aid' and states that: 'Every regulating rein aid must end with a yielding of the reins [and] ...must not end up as a "pulling" on the reins. A prolonged pull on the reins would only cause the horse to lean on the bit rather than to yield to the rein aid.'[22] Sylvia Loch says: 'The feeling of take and give is made by the fingers through a very gentle squeezing or vibrato on the rein.'[23] Jane Savoie: 'Straighten him by lightly vibrating, squeezing/releasing, or pulsing your fingers on the inside rein.'[24] These great masters are all explaining 'pressure-reaction-release'. It is a foolproof method of teaching horses to yield to pressure and riders to yield to the horse's correct reaction. This is not possible if the hands do not move.

The rule of thumb is to be hard when the horse is hard and soft when the horse is soft. *This does not mean that riders should be harsh* – It means that the rider should relax or 'soften' (yield) to reward the horse immediately he yields to finger pressure. Every small correct yielding by the horse should be rewarded. This encourages him to yield sooner and better the next time.

When learning the technique of 'take and give' with only the fingers, novice riders often tighten and lock the entire arm in co-contraction. This causes resistance and blocks forward movement. Co-contraction soon dissipates when the new coordinated pattern of movement is practised correctly.

All the complicated and even gag bits (which are not allowed in dressage competitions) on the market are evidence that riders are not taught the correct techniques of communicating through their hands and fingers (or legs). Correctly applied, this pressure-release system works immediately. Riders with good feel master it in a very short time. Within three lessons all mouth and resistance problems disappear. Riders have to learn how to give effective pressure and to yield instantly as the horse yields, and horses have to be taught to yield to light pressure. Riders have to develop a significant vocabulary through finger, hand and sometimes even arm pressures. When riders are taught to use their hands correctly, together with how to use their legs to control the horse, the need for strong bits will disappear completely. The end product of 'take and give' is invisible hand and finger aids. Thus form follows function.

Chapter 11

HAND USE – TECHNIQUE AND TIMING

Riders' hands and fingers have no other responsibility than to communicate with the horse through the reins. The hands and fingers have to give clear, unambiguous explanations. These many messages should become so delicate and light that they are invisible.

DETRIMENTAL HAND AND FINGER MOVEMENTS

Riders who lack awareness, feel and timing, misunderstand and use the pressure-release techniques incorrectly. Horses misunderstand these riders. Incorrect hand use blocking forward movement results in confusion, a hard mouth, resistance or a lack of impulsion in the horse. Horses will react correctly the first time you ask if your hand and finger techniques are correct. Immediate success is an important barometer which prevents confusion in the horse.

   Hardness in hand use may be situated in the rider's elbows, shoulder joints and even the shoulder girdle, but it affects the whole arm. The following hand actions are hard and detrimental to the horse:

1. Harsh movements and snatching or jerking on the reins (usually with large movements) cause sharp pain and should never be used.

2. Continuous and strong contact by holding, setting or locking of the arms and

hands is a misunderstanding of contact. It causes discomfort, numbs the mouth, causes nerve damage, a hard mouth and blocks forward movement.

3. Elbow or shoulder rigidity or hands 'doing nothing' with a continuous hold, have no elasticity. They cause discomfort and an opposing hanging from the horse.

4. Rein-pulling and hanging always result in resistance. The horse lifts his head or pulls. It is counterproductive and has no place in equitation.

5. Riders may, purely by luck, have a small element of success with one type of squeezing on the reins. This encourages them to continue using the same repetitive finger, hand or arm actions, often with little or no useful result. The habit soon degenerates into either continual fiddling of the type described in Chapter 6, or actual sawing.

6. Sawing constitutes the horse's head being simply pulled from side to side. The pressure is not a request for the horse to yield and there is no reward if/when the horse does yield. Sawing soon degenerates into rhythmic, repetitive, left-right movement with the hands, which may become literally mindless on the rider's part. Horses will maintain the round flexor frame with their heads in mid-position when they yield to bit pressure, so do not get 'stuck' in repetitive squeezes when the outcome is not correct.

GOOD HANDS

One of the greatest compliments a rider can receive is, 'You have good hands.' What then, are good hands? The hands form the connection between the reins and the arms. Good hands are therefore good arms because it is arm tightness which blocks elasticity. Good arms and hands avoid undue pressure on the bit, a major cause of restricted head and neck movements. The arms yield when the horse yields. They move forward and back with the horse's mouth/head and neck as they communicate effectively through the bit. They always have a giving/yielding feeling towards the horse's mouth, never a fixed stillness. Erik Herbermann notes the importance of 'The need to have a clear forward-pushing *attitude* with both hands most of the time – especially after every rein aid.'[1] The horse's neck must always be allowed to move away from, not scrunch up towards, the rider's hands. This ensures a consistent soft, elastic contact. Momentary locking of the arms into co-contraction (*not* pulling back) may be needed in a few specific situations only.

> THINK OF 'giving the reins back to the horse' almost like offering canapés on a tray.

An independent seat is the cornerstone and prerequisite of good hands and independent rein communication. Lack of core stability, good muscle tone and sufficient gross and fine motor coordination skills is a major problem in hand use. It causes every rein action to have a tendency to pull.

Good hands and fingers never have a fixed stillness. They are alive with gentle movement to prevent habituation and 'deadness'. They feel every nuance from the horse's mouth, then constantly act and react, adjusting the contact with delicate and sophisticated feather-light finger pressures (almost nuances of pressure) – invisible tweaks on the reins. Communication through the bit will be gentle, preventing the horse from reacting incorrectly. Light, meaningful movements of the hand, or pressure from the fingers, are all trained horses need to react. This reaction may be simply about being more alert, softening the contact, flexing, or bending the neck. Only the horse and rider will be aware of these light pressures.

DEVELOPING 'QUIET/STILL' HANDS

Hands *appear* to be 'quiet'/'still'/'steady'/'carried' when they move with the horse's mouth, head and neck. This is only possible when the arms, hands and fingers are relaxed and devoid of stiffness and tension. Follow these steps to develop quiet hands.

1. Hold a piece of mane, with both hands, in front of the withers, the reins loose. Feel your arms move back and forth and your shoulder joints open and close as the horse walks.

2. Most riders seem to instinctively tighten their arm muscles when they ask the horse to move off from the halt. This gives him a 'stop' message as he is asked to go. The arms should yield slightly forwards when the horse is asked to take a forward step.

3. Remove the tension in your arms by setting them up for correct learning. The best method of relaxing your elbows during rising trot is to rest your knuckles or pinkies and maintain constant contact on the horse's withers. This forces your arms to relax and your elbows to open and close as your body rises and drops. Become aware of this open and closed feeling (see photo on page 153).
    a. Maintain this until your arm muscles have developed the memory of relaxation. If need be, press down on your knuckles until the tendency to tighten your arm disappears.
    b. If your arms are short, you may have to temporarily lean a little too far forwards. However, this slight positional fault will correct itself when your arms and hands relax into correct use.

c. If the problem improves, but is not eradicated, you can hold onto a piece of mane or a strap tied to the D-rings of the saddle. I usually remove the flash strap from the bridle, since it serves very little purpose, and fix this to both D-rings. Hold very lightly onto this. Hanging on for balance will defeat the object.

These exercises will lead to hands which appear quiet and do not pull on horses' mouths. Here again, form follows function.

The difference between restraining rein aids and asking the horse to yield

The reins are used to restrain the horse as well as to ask him to yield into the round flexor, 'on the bit' frame. This could be confusing for horses, but clear differences between these two instructions avoid confusion. The restraining aid incorporates locking of the elbows; it blocks all forward movement. When the horse is trained correctly, restraining hand aids are quickly transferred to knee pressure alone as explained in Chapter 7.

The aid to yield into a round flexor frame is a soft aid of finger vibration or squeezing: the elbows remaining soft. This aid is often used together with bend. Once the horse is yielding, the bit does not cause stopping pressure. Horses lose impulsion when both hands, used together, mean 'stop' as well as 'yield'.

Functions of the individual hands

The inside hand

The inside hand indicates and maintains the bend and the bent-straight position. Small fluttering/feathering/vibrating movements ensure a light yielding contact and a true bend in which the horse uses his own muscles. It is always accompanied by pressure from the inside leg, which pushes the horse's ribcage to produce bend. The inside leg is used first, followed by the hand aid. (In fact, the more effectively the inside leg is used, the less inside hand will be necessary to maintain bend; horses eventually learn to bend from leg pressure alone.) The inside hand and fingers initially have few completely static moments. The hand and fingers should be alive, feeling and acting continuously to communicate the rider's wishes to the horse.

The outside hand

The outside hand moves the horse's shoulders by moving closer to or further from them. The outside arm and hand contact is usually fairly steady provided the horse has a correct inside bend. However, if a horse is resistant to yielding or lifts his head and neck, the outside hand may be used together with the inside hand, or with alternating pressure-release actions.

REIN AID TECHNIQUES AND USES

All rein aids are variations of finger or hand pressure and the release of pressure, all of which the horse experiences through the bit. They are mostly accompanied by the appropriate leg and weight aids in the correct sequence, although the tiny finger movements of the 'early warning system' do not need to be accompanied by leg aids.

All rein aids must remain meaningful. The correct pressure-release rein technique is to tweak, squeeze or hold the reins until the horse yields – or sometimes *begins to yield*. The hold is not a pull, but a passive resistance, followed by the reward of an instant release in which the rein is given back to the horse as he yields. A tickle on the withers will reinforce the reward.

Finger and hand aids can be executed with differing sequences of pressure with either one hand, alternate hands or both hands together, depending on the message you intend to convey. There are no hard and fast rules. It is about feeling when and where the appropriate pressure is needed as you feel slight pressure changes of the rein on your ring finger or your arm. Provided the horse's mouth has not been corrupted and your contact is elastic and soft, all you will need are light finger tweaks/vibrations for a yielding reaction. This is the ideal. Once a horse has developed a mouth problem, the intensity and frequency of finger and hand actions may have to increase to squeezing, sponging, squeezing harder or for longer, stronger vibrations, momentarily making a fist and holding it until the horse yields, flexing the wrists and locking your elbows. Practise and experiment with the pressure technique variations described in the following pages.

Note that, although the rein aids have been separated into two sub-sections, they all form a unit. Riders have to learn to feel when one-handed, alternate or two-handed rein pressure is needed. The rein aids are described in order of light to strong pressure. The myriad possibilities of hand and finger aids described in this chapter may appear to promote/suggest an overuse of the hands. However, the exercises and examples are all to teach technique and timing. This leads to exquisitely light hand or finger pressures, which is the goal. Only if light aids are not effective do you experiment to find the pressure which the horse understands immediately. If you train your horse with a yielding, soft contact from the outset, you will need very few hand aids and they will not be strong.

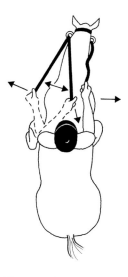

The outside straight rein moves the shoulders while the inside rein remains soft.

A HORSE I SCHOOL intermittently had been jumped and schooled in tight running reins. This system of simultaneous hand and leg use caused defensive behaviour. His new owner follows the hands without legs and legs without hands system, which lessened his defensive behaviour. At the start of every session he pulls or hangs on my hands, or he curls his neck to evade the pressure, but after fifteen minutes his contact becomes perfectly soft, and his lightness consistent. He also maintains it for his owner. Unfortunately he also is ridden by a selection of other riders who do not use this system. He thus has a continuing pattern of reverting to his defensive contact behaviour until it is schooled out of him again. The point, though, is that it only takes fifteen minutes to correct and revert to soft finger vibrations if the rider uses the correct techniques.

One-handed and alternate rein aids

Bend is an extremely important aspect of training horses. It improves almost all riding movements. Bend, especially on the stiff side, breaks the tight extensor pattern of the entire spine, thus assisting in maintaining the flexor frame. It is therefore easier for horses to understand yielding into the round flexor frame through single or alternate rein aids. Bending in the direction of the movement is the major difference between schooling movements and the horse's natural movements.

ON THE SUBJECT of bend, it is useful to know that it is extremely difficult for horses to rear or buck when their necks are yielding to one side. They need the extensor pattern and equal balance on both hind legs to rear.

The following notes and exercises relate to one-handed or alternating rein aids. Two-handed rein aids are discussed separately, but they may have to follow single-handed aids – some are, therefore, also included in this section.

1. Your finger and hand movements should be softly alive, feeling and acting continuously as the communication requires, to prevent habituation and a heavy contact. Molly Sivewright says: 'The ring finger of one or other hand should keep up a softly murmuring vibration with one side of the horse's mouth or the other whilst the horse remains straight or when positioned, turning, flexing or bending to the left or to the right.'[2]

2. These aids can be used as an 'early warning system' – catch the horse's attention and prepare him for every movement with either inside or alternate finger-feathering a few strides into the movement. This explains that he should not tighten his neck for balance. Few riders explain clearly to the horse the next step he should take. He is thus often 'caught by surprise and off balance' going into the next movement. This is one of the reasons why novice riders often cannot maintain a steady contact. *Compare this to using your indicator to warn the other drivers that a turn is imminent.*

   One of the 'early warning' functions of this aid is, in fact, to initiate and encourage head and neck bend to the inside for circles, turns, shoulder-in and half-pass with feathering well before the movement. Feathering is especially effective during small circles on the horse's stiff side. It prevents loss of balance and maintains soft bend. Inside leg pressure should always precede this feathering.

3. Light closing of individual fingers (usually the ring finger of one or alternate hands, as with typing or playing the piano quietly) while the arms remain yielding, is the ideal mild control which should be enough to communicate all intentions to the horse. It is a refinement of 'take and give' – the finished product of invisible communication. Horses understand this once they have learnt to yield to pressure. Such aids can be used for many purposes, for example:

   a. To actually indicate direction – point the horse's nose in the new direction and maintain it on your aiming point with further light squeezes, as necessary.

   b. To ask the horse to lower his neck by using alternate or inside hand soft squeezes and releases. Yield as he responds correctly.

   c. To maintain a consistent round flexor 'on the bit' frame. Soft squeezes of the inside rein or alternate feathering should explain the exact contact desired and pre-empt or correct head-lifting when the horse loses attention. Also use these actions to correct tendencies for the horse to lean on the reins or move onto the forehand.

   d. To prevent the horse from using his neck for balance through transitions. Use alternate soft finger squeezes/feathering, or squeeze the inside rein (especially when this is the horse's stiff side) to prevent loss of bend and head-lifting.

4. Alternating pressure from the whole hand (squeezing or sponging) on the reins may be used when the horse is not responsive to light squeezing. This may take the form of sponging once on each side, or twice on one side and once on the other, or any other sequence, depending on the increase of pressure on one or

above left Squeeze the inside rein to ask the horse to yield. Note horse's ear focusing on rider's hand.

above right Release the pressure as the horse yields. (Note the inside neck muscles contracting and the bend affecting the reins.)

other ring finger. There is no recipe: it is about feeling where the horse is tightening the incorrect muscles. The intensity of this sponging depends on the horse's reaction speed to yielding. Some examples of when to use this type of pressure are as follows:

a. When teaching a young horse to lengthen the trot you can prevent loss of balance by using light alternating hand pressure to maintain the flexor frame and rhythm throughout. As he takes even a slightly stronger rein his balance changes and he will start to move wide behind, lose balance and rhythm, speed up or break into canter. You have to react by squeezing as you feel the slightest tightening on your ring finger. Only when horses can lengthen in their own balance without leaning on the reins, can the contact become firmer to produce an eye-catching extended trot.

b. To perfect lengthening at walk. It will then automatically be correct at the trot and canter. Ask the horse to stretch down by yielding both reins forwards. As he starts to take the reins out of your hands, close your hands, either simultaneously or alternately, to prevent him from snatching or pulling. Then slip both reins a little. Repeat the squeeze and release until his neck is fully stretched. If you simply let the reins go, the horse learns to pull them out of your hands first and then lifts his head and neck. Maintain the stretch with soft alternate vibrations.

HORSES IN NATURE hold the round flexor frame for less than a minute at a time, and this frame is held for only a few minutes in a dressage test. Holding it longer causes discomfort and possible damage to the joints and soft tissue around the joints of the neck. It is important that horses stretch regularly during work – every time they have done a good movement.

c. To shorten the frame after extended walk. Gather the reins, little by little, one then the other. Squeeze each rein as you gather it, to ask the horse to remain yielding.

d. When a horse canters too fast in a hollow, extended frame, take with one hand and hold. Take with the other hand. Then release both hands forward simultaneously to form loops in the reins. Allow the horse to lengthen his frame and drop his head and neck down. Use this sequence in the canter rhythm over three canter strides. You will see that the horse's rhythm slows down, the canter balance improves and you learn not to hang on when the horse speeds up. Hanging on in canter is counterproductive: the horse goes faster. The intensity of this 'take and give' depends on the horse's reaction. This technique works especially well for retraining retired racehorses, or horses with spoilt mouths. You can also use it together with a half-halt, then give the reins forward.

Release the reins forward to form loops to slow down the canter.

5. Momentary hold and release of one rein, mostly the inside, by forming a fist, is used when the horse is resistant to lighter squeezes. This is the proverbial 'squeezing all the water from a sponge' movement. Use this to prevent the horse from lifting his head into transitions, if a lighter aid is not effective. Hold your fist and wait for the horse to yield, then release the pressure instantly.

6. Strong closing of one fist, together with setting the arm, is sometimes needed when a horse resists bending. Lock your hand on the horse's withers or the saddle to ensure that it does not move. Hold and wait until the horse solves the problem by yielding, then release instantly. Wrist flexing may be used if the horse is a little resistant. Release as the horse yields.

7. The outside hand and arm move and control the horse's shoulders with a slightly firmer and steadier contact than that of the inside rein. Uses/effects of this hand and arm are as follows:

   a. A firm contact on an opening outside rein moves the shoulder out. Take your outside arm out and a little back to straighten the rein. Maintain the inside bend with vibrations on the inside rein and a pushing inside leg as you move the shoulders out. If the outside rein is loose you will not be successful.

   b. Control the shoulders to prevent them from 'falling in' by opening the outside rein away from the horse's shoulder together with inside leg pressure and stepping out.

   c. Indicate the size of the circles, the angle of shoulder-in and half-passes with a firm outside contact. Move your outside hand closer to, or open it away from the horse's shoulders, as the size of the circle or angle dictates (see also photo on page 120).

   d. The outside rein maintains and regulates the contact for the correct inside bend in circles, shoulder-in, half-pass, canter depart and canter pirouette. This is the ideal and, together with a soft inside rein, is proof of a correct inside bend.

   e. Move your outside hand towards your inside hip to move the horse's shoulder in, or to prevent it from 'popping/falling out'. When horses are reluctant to move their shoulders, a significant amount of pressure may be needed. Horses tend to hug the wall, on one side, when learning the shoulder-in. You may need strong tension on the outside rein by crossing it over the withers, towards your inside hip, to convince an impervious horse to move his shoulders off the track. One of the main reasons why riders have difficulty in moving the horse's shoulders into the shoulder-in position is that they have been taught that the hand should never cross the withers. However, it is your inside hand which should not cross the withers for bend, or to move the horse's shoulders out. When the inside hand crosses the withers it creates excessive bend. This action does not move the horse's shoulders out or prevent 'falling in'; it blocks forward movement and causes the horse's nose to tilt. It often becomes a useless habit, especially on the rider's non-dominant side. It is a strange habit because it cannot achieve the desired result. It is far more effective and easier to simply open the outside rein to move the horse's shoulders out and prevent 'falling in'.

In her first lesson this rider's inside hand crossed the withers in an attempt to prevent 'falling in' while riding a circle, but it only pulled the horse's neck in. Note the lack of muscle definition in the neck.

below The photo shows the detail of the same rider's lack of coordination, with her inside (left) hand crossing the horse's withers in her second lesson.

left By her third lesson she could ask the horse for bend with light finger pressure alone. Note the contraction of the horse's neck muscles.

    f. Use both arms together, with your knuckles touching, to move the horse's shoulders during the shoulder-in, half-pass or when the horse is 'falling in'. Retard the lateral steps of the forelimbs by moving both hands slightly to the outside when the horse's shoulders move sideways too fast in half-pass. Move both hands closer to the track to close the shoulder-in angle to 30 degrees when it becomes too large. Move both hands to the inside to enlarge the angle when it becomes too small.

    g. Control the shoulders on the straight lines across the diagonal and down the centre line into the halt. Maintain identical contact and point the horse's nose on the marker while pushing the horse forwards, for only these two lines.

8. An opening inside rein leads the horse's shoulders to the inside. Use it to initiate the walk pirouette. This may only be needed on the horse's 'stiff' side.

9. It may be necessary, when training young horses or retraining spoilt horses, to open both arms to encourage the horse to lower his head and neck.

    a. Horses seem to understand better to lower their necks when riders open both arms, in a low position. It also encourages the flexor pattern.

    b. This position, together with alternating hand squeezes followed by slipping the reins when the horse yields, teaches the young horse to stretch his head and neck forwards and down. It may initially be necessary to lean forwards and stretch your arms down next to the horse's shoulders, if the horse does not understand the concept, or if you are not effective with your hands in the normal position. It may also be necessary to use this method when correcting previous schooling errors. This stretching is very important for horses with back problems such as kissing spines, and as a reward after collected work.

10. The head-lifting aid is used only when horses pull or hang down on the reins. They should be left in a low and round position if the contact is light. Young horses often seem to be more comfortable in this low neck-carriage; it is probably to rest their developing muscles. This low carriage lifts automatically as the correct muscles develop. Incorrectly schooled horses often take up this position during re-schooling; it seems to be a protective defence position to prevent being pulled in the mouth. When these horses feel confident that the bit won't hurt, they will move into a higher head and neck carriage automatically.

    Whether they are young, or in need of re-schooling, it is not a good idea to lift horses' necks before their muscles and confidence develop sufficiently for a higher head and neck carriage. However, when a horse pulls down on the reins, a one-handed lift with contact (usually the outside hand), will convince him to lift his neck. This action should be released as he lifts his head. It may hollow the horse momentarily, but the round frame is quickly regained. Lifting the rein may also cause loss of impulsion if the horse perceives it as a half-halt or halt signal, or a blocking agent. However, carrying both hands high, in an attempt to solve the problem, either lifts and 'shortens' the horse's neck, or reinforces the pull, losing lightness or the correct round flexor frame.

11. Use alternate stopping rein pressure to control the exact stride length of each foreleg during half steps, collected walk and piaffe. Release the rein pressure to reward the correct response as the horse shortens his steps.

One-handed lift to ask the horse not to pull down.

Using both hands together

Simultaneous two-handed restraint generally results in resistant head-lifting and resistance to slowing down, especially if the restraint is prolonged. This is often seen during jumping when inexperienced riders attempt to slow down their horses. However, once horses have learnt to yield to bit pressure and are obedient to stopping off leg aids, two-handed half-halts can be used. The two-handed aids can be used in the following ways.

1. Close the fingers of both hands lightly and hold momentarily as the horse starts tightening his topline to lift his head. This is experienced as a slightly stronger contact. Release as he yields.

2. A stronger two-handed response of closing the fists can also be used as the horse begins to lose the round flexor frame. It will not be visible if the horse yields immediately. Timing of the pressure and release has to be correct in order for the horse to maintain a consistent round frame.

3. Some horses have developed such defensive resistance or insensitivity to bit pressure that they need special training to learn the concept of yielding into the soft flexor frame or bending the neck. In this case we give the horse a pressure problem to solve. The principle of this technique is the same as tying a horse to tie rings or riding with non-elastic side-reins. When he cannot pull away, he solves the problem by yielding to the pressure. The major difference in this scenario is that the pressure can be released completely and the horse can be given complete freedom of his neck without consistent restriction. Once a horse understands yielding to bit pressure and the rider maintains a yielding contact, the horse learns to trust the rider's hands and the defensive resistance disappears. The alternative of continuous nagging is most detrimental to the horse's well-being.

Jean Licart explained this technique as follows:

> This is accomplished by closing the fingers on the reins and by setting the hands. The rider tightens his fingers to the point of crushing the reins if necessary, but without drawing back his elbows the slightest bit. His arms should be 'arms of steel', with all their muscles set … Setting his hands as if the wrists were bolted to the saddle.[3]

This is co-contraction of the arms. Strong men seem to be able to set their arms as Licart explains, preventing the horse from moving their hands forwards, but most women have to anchor their hands with downward pressure in position on the horse's neck, withers, saddle or even their own thighs. Downward pressure is important to prevent you from pulling in opposition to the horse's strong neck muscles.

Start the exercise at halt. Use a momentarily stronger 'hold and release'. You can use your inside hand or, if that does not have the desired effect, you may use both hands. If the horse does not yield, strengthen your hold on the rein and tighten your arm in co-contraction. *Do not pull back.* If you pull back, the horse can pull your arms forwards. He will learn to resist more. This anchor ensures that the pressure remains consistent and prevents the horse from moving your hands forwards. It is a *passive resistance.* If you restrain without a point of reference, the horse will be able to pull your arms slightly forwards. Even a very slight forward movement (1cm) releases the bit pressure and rewards the horse for pulling, thus encouraging him to pull more (*he* will be teaching *you* to yield). This reinforcement of pulling retards the learning process. He has to figure out

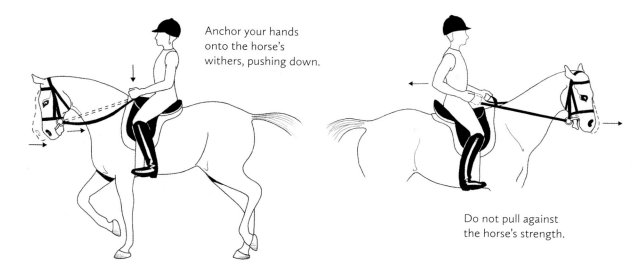

Anchor your hands onto the horse's withers, pushing down.

Do not pull against the horse's strength.

that correct yielding on his part will remove the pressure. The harder the horse resists and the slower he is to yield, the tighter your hands should be as you push down and wait for him to solve the problem.

When the horse figures out that he can relieve the pressure by yielding, release the pressure immediately and completely. Do not yield before the horse has reacted correctly. You will need this strong pressure only once or twice, provided you release the pressure immediately, after which the horse will yield immediately when you apply light finger pressure on the reins.

4. Momentary locking of both the elbows.
   a. Lock your elbows momentarily together with alternate feathering of the reins into the halt. The need for the restraining elbow-locking disappears when the horse is obedient to stopping from knee pressure alone. The horse finally moves off only leg aids and soft finger vibrations into the correct 'on the bit' halt (see Chapter 7).
   b. Lock your elbows momentarily together with alternate feathering of the reins for the on-the-bit rein-back. Locked elbows explain to the horse that he should not step forwards. Alternate rein-feathering explains to the horse that he should maintain the round flexor frame throughout the rein-back. Release your elbows to reward him as he steps back. The need for finger pressure disappears when the horse understands and is obedient to the rein-back. Alternate leg pressure explains to the horse that he should step backwards.

5. Half-halts.
   a. Use a two-handed half-halt a split second after knee pressure, to regulate balance, tempo and rhythm. 'Catch' the impulsion when the horse is moving

too fast by momentarily locking both elbows and simultaneously squeezing alternate reins to prevent the horse from lifting his head. Release the pressure as the horse slows down. Repeat this half-halt at the first sign of increasing rhythm. You will eventually need only knee pressure and finger vibrations for this slowing down half-halt.

b. Restrain the horse momentarily by tightening both or alternate hands and elbows a little to 'catch' too big a forward step. Release the pressure as the horse takes smaller steps. Add calf pressure for more engagement to ensure that the horse does not lose impulsion. Repeat as necessary to maintain shorter steps.

c. 'Lift' the horse off his forehand in canter with half-halts using knee pressure, both hands and elbows together with finger vibrations, followed instantly by calf pressure. Also stretch your upper body and pinch your seat muscles together with the half-halt and then release all pressure. Do this at every stride of the canter.

d. Engage and collect the horse by using two-handed half-halts split seconds after knee pressure to catch the energy produced by your leg and seat aids. As the horse engages his hindquarters with a higher step, yield your hands forwards. Repeat the process at every stride to control the quality of collection. Steinbrecht recommends, 'Use your hands to transfer its [the horse's] weight to the hindquarters.'[4]

   (When the horse is bending correctly to the inside, you may need only to use your outside hand to half-halt.)

6. Instant locking of the hands and elbows while pushing down on the withers when the horse snatches the reins. This should be done as the horse begins to snatch. He will bump himself against the bit and realise that snatching is not a good idea. Horses have a preamble to this snatching. They either first lift and drop their heads, or they nod. The snatch follows immediately. You have to lock your arms during the preamble to the snatch. *It is important to release the reins instantly he responds to reward the horse, then to maintain soft contact to take away his reason for snatching.* Even 10-year-old children are able to learn how to prevent their ponies from snatching. Horses snatch to get relief from the pressure of continuous contact on their mouths, or to rest their tired neck flexor muscles.

ONE OF MY PET hates is when riders, sitting at rest, keep their horses 'on the bit'. One can often see the horses trying desperately to stretch. When you stop to talk to your trainer or friends, be courteous and release the rein pressure to allow your horse the same freedom you allow yourself.

CONCLUSION

THIS BOOK COMPLETES the trilogy of my books which covers all aspects of training horses and teaching riders. *Equine Biomechanics for Riders – The Key to Balanced Riding* explains how the horse's body works, which knowledge enables us to school him logically. *Successful Schooling – Train Your Horse with Empathy* teaches the rider how to train the horse, and this book is concerned with rider biomechanics and effective body use in communicating with horses.

The golden thread running through these books is understanding. The rider has to understand the trainer and the horse has to understand the rider. Confusion leads to slow learning and rigidity in both horse and rider. The rider's ability to use every body part independently and also to coordinate the parts as necessary is essential for clear communication. My wish is that these books will ensure that horses and riders do not have to go through all the ineffective communication techniques before finally finding the language horses understand with ease.

Being prey animals, horses have never needed to stalk their food, therefore there has been little evolution of their cognitive skills. They learn through memory. Furthermore, the same biomechanical principles apply to all horses. As long as the training techniques and exercises are applied according to sound biomechanical principles and learning theory, they should lead to correct results. When exercises or methods of riding contravene these principles, they often lead to damage despite the fashion of the day. Rhetoric, even that passed down through many years, does not necessarily make a method correct. All statements and claims have to be tested by the laws of biomechanics.

Riders should forget about the end product and follow the basic exercises in the book. These, with their emphasis on coordination and body use, should automatically and naturally correct most communication problems between horse and rider. This leads to good rhythm and balance, suppleness, and the correct round flexor frame. Riders then become one with the horse and ride in harmony, with the lightest possible aids and pressures.

REFERENCES

Introduction
1. Jean Saint-Fort Paillard, *Understanding Equitation*, Doubleday & Company Inc. (Pitman Publishing Ltd.), Great Britain, 1975.
2. Ibid.

Chapter 2
1. Dr Thomas Ritter, *Dressage Principles Based on Biomechanics*, Cadmos Publishing Ltd, UK, 2011.
2. Hilda Nelson, *Alexis-François L'Hotte The Quest for Lightness in Equitation*, J.A. Allen, London, 1997.
3. Dr Thomas Ritter, *Dressage Principles Based on Biomechanics*, Cadmos Publishing Ltd, UK, 2011.

Chapter 3
1. Hilda Nelson, *Alexis-François L'Hotte The Quest for Lightness in Equitation*, J.A. Allen, London, 1997.
2. Ibid.
3. Wilhelm Müseler, *Riding Logic*, Methuen & Co. London, 1937 (1966 edn).
4. Gustav Steinbrecht, *The Gymnasium of the Horse*, Xenophon Press, Ohio, 1995.
5. Charlene Strickland, *Western Riding*, R.R. Donnelley, USA, 1995.
6. Penny Hillsdon, *Pathfinder Dressage*, J.A Allen, London, 2000.
7. Gustav Steinbrecht, *The Gymnasium of the Horse*, Xenophon Press, Ohio, 1995.
8. Gustav Steinbrecht, *The Gymnasium of the Horse*, Xenophon Press, Ohio, 1995.
9. Nuno Oliveira, *Reflections on Equestrian Art*, J.A. Allen, London, 1976.

Chapter 4
1. Peter M. McGinnis, *Biomechanics of Sport and Exercise*, Library of Congress, USA, 1999.
2. Hilda Nelson, *Alexis François L'Hotte The Quest for Lightness in Equitation*, J.A. Allen, 1997.
3. Hilda Nelson, *Alexis François L'Hotte The Quest for Lightness in Equitation*, J.A. Allen, 1997.
4. Hilda Nelson, *Alexis François L'Hotte The Quest for Lightness in Equitation*, J.A. Allen, London, 1997.
5. Xenophon, *On Horsemanship*, (trans. H.G. Dakyns), John Bickers, and David Widger, E-book, 2008.
6. You can read more about conditioning in Andrew McLean's *The Truth About Horses*, David & Charles, Devon, 2003.

Chapter 5
1. Patricia M. Davies, *Steps to Follow*, Springer-Verlag, Berlin, 1985.
2. Sally Swift, *Centered Riding 2 Further Exploration*, J.A. Allen, London, 2002.

Chapter 6
1. E.C. Merchant (trans. G.W. Bowerstock), *Xenophon In Seven Volumes, Constitution of the Athenians*, Harvard University Press, Cambridge, MA.
2. Nuno Oliveira, *Reflections on Equestrian Art*, J.A. Allen, London, 1976.
3. Jean Claude Racinet, *Falling for Fallacies*, Cadmos Books, UK, 2009.

Chapter 8
1. Wilhelm Müseler, *Riding Logic* (trans. F.W. Schiller), Methuen & Co. Ltd. (third edn), London, 1965.
2. *The Concise Oxford Dictionary*, Oxford University Press.
3. Wilhelm Müseler, *Riding Logic* (trans. F.W. Schiller), Methuen & Co. Ltd. (third edn), London, 1965.

Chapter 10
1. Nuno Oliveira, *Reflections on Equestrian Art*, J.A. Allen, London, 1976.
2. Gustav Steinbrecht, *The Gymnasium of the Horse*, Xenophon Press, Ohio, 1995.
3. Gustav Steinbrecht, *The Gymnasium of the Horse*, Xenophon Press, Ohio, 1995.
4. Hilda Nelson, *Alexis-François L'Hotte The Quest for Lightness in Equitation*, J.A. Allen, London, 1997.
5. William Cavendish, Duke of Newcastle, *A General System*

of Horsemanship,(1st edn France, 1658), J.A Allen, London, 1970.

6. Hilda Nelson, *Alexis-François L'Hotte, The Quest for Lightness in Equitation*, J.A. Allen, London, 1997.

7. Nuno Oliveira, *Reflections on Equestrian Art*, J.A. Allen, London, 1976.

8. Michel Henriquet and Catherine Durand, *Henriquet on Dressage*, (trans. Hilda Nelson), J.A. Allen, London, 2004.

9. Tineke Bartels, *Riding with Awareness and Feel*, J.A. Allen, London, 2008.

10. Tineke Bartels, *Riding with Awareness and Feel*, J.A. Allen, London, 2008.

11. Ibid.

12. Gustav Steinbrecht, *The Gymnasium of the Horse*, Xenophon Press, Ohio, 1995.

13. Xenophon, *The Art of Horsemanship* (trans. M.H. Morgan Ph.D), J.A. Allen, London, 1962.

14. François Robichon de la Guérinière, *School of Horsemanship* (trans.Tracy Boucher), J.A. Allen, London, 1993.

15. Hilda Nelson, *François Baucher, The Man and His Method*, J.A Allen, London, 1992.

16. Gustav Steinbrecht, *The Gymnasium of the Horse*, Xenophon Press, Ohio, 1995.

17. James Fillis, *Breaking and Riding*, J.A. Allen, London, 1973.

18. Alois Podhajsky, *The Complete Training of Horse and Rider*, George G. Harrap & Co. Ltd., London, 1967.

19. Anthony Paalman, *Training Showjumpers*, J.A. Allen, London, 1978.

20. Nuno Oliveira, *Notes and Reminiscences of a Portuguese Rider*, J.A. Allen, 1982.

21. Molly Sivewright, *Thinking Riding*, J.A Allen & Co. London 1984.

22. *The Principles of Riding, Official Handbook of the German Equestrian Federation*, Threshold Books Ltd., London, 1990.

23. Sylvia Loch, *Dressage in Lightness*, J.A. Allen, London, 2000.

24. Jane Savoie, *Cross-Train Your Horse – Book 1*, Trafalgar Square Books, Vermont, 1998.

Chapter 11

1. Erik Herbermann, *A Horseman's Notes*, p.77, Core Publishing, USA, 2003.

2. Molly Sivewright, *Thinking Riding*, J.A. Allen, London, 1984.

3. Jean Licart, *Basic Equitation*, J.A. Allen, London, 1966.

4. Gustav Steinbrecht, *The Gymnasium of the Horse*, Xenophon Press, Ohio, 1995.

INDEX